# C# for Object-Oriented Programming: Unlock the Power of OOP

## A Comprehensive Guide to Mastering C# and Object-Oriented Design

MIGUEL FARMER

RAFAEL SANDERS

Table of Content

# *TABLE OF CONTENTS*

# INTRODUCTION

Welcome to **"C# for Object-Oriented Programming: Unlock the Power of OOP"**—your comprehensive guide to mastering **C#** and **Object-Oriented Programming (OOP)**. Whether you're a beginner eager to dive into the world of C# or an experienced developer looking to refine your skills, this book offers an in-depth exploration of C# concepts, coupled with clear explanations of **OOP principles** that will elevate your software design and development abilities.

*Why Object-Oriented Programming?*

Object-Oriented Programming (OOP) is a programming paradigm that is based on the concept of **objects**—data structures that combine both **state** (attributes) and **behavior** (methods). Unlike procedural programming, which focuses on a sequence of instructions, OOP emphasizes modeling real-world entities and their interactions. This approach allows developers to create more **modular**, **scalable**, and **maintainable** code.

The benefits of OOP are clear:

- **Reusability**: Through inheritance, we can create new classes based on existing ones, avoiding code duplication.
- **Maintainability**: OOP allows changes to be made in one place without affecting the entire codebase.

6

- **Modularity**: Code is structured into self-contained objects, making it easier to understand, test, and maintain.
- **Abstraction**: OOP allows us to hide complex implementation details and expose only necessary information, leading to cleaner interfaces.

By mastering C# and its implementation of OOP, you are equipping yourself with the skills to build robust applications that can grow and evolve with changing requirements.

*The Journey Ahead*

This book is designed to guide you through the concepts of C#, OOP, and the tools you need to design, build, and maintain real-world applications. Here's how we'll take you through your learning journey:

1. **Foundations of C# and OOP**: We begin by exploring the core concepts of **C#** and how it supports **Object-Oriented Programming**. We'll look at the essentials of C# syntax and how to build classes, objects, and work with fundamental OOP concepts like **encapsulation**, **inheritance**, **polymorphism**, and **abstraction**.
2. **SOLID Principles**: You'll learn how to design your code in a way that is **modular**, **flexible**, and **maintainable** by adhering to the **SOLID** principles. These five

7

principles—**Single Responsibility, Open/Closed, Liskov Substitution, Interface Segregation,** and **Dependency Inversion**—will guide you to write software that is easy to extend and change without breaking existing functionality.

3. **Advanced C# Features**: We'll dive into advanced features like **nullable types, tuples,** and **pattern matching,** helping you harness the full power of C# and write clean, efficient, and modern code.

4. **Working with APIs**: Real-world applications often rely on interacting with external data sources. We'll teach you how to make HTTP requests, work with **RESTful APIs,** and handle responses using JSON, giving you the skills to integrate your applications with the world around them.

5. **Unit Testing and Test-Driven Development (TDD)**: In this book, you'll learn the importance of writing tests for your code. Through **unit testing** and **Test-Driven Development,** we'll show you how to ensure that your software behaves as expected and how to refactor with confidence.

6. **Building Real-World Applications**: Finally, we bring everything together by walking through the creation of a real-world application, from **design** to **deployment.** This project will serve as a capstone where you apply all the concepts and techniques you've learned throughout the book.

*How This Book Is Structured*

The book is broken down into **27 chapters**, each focused on a key area of C# and Object-Oriented Programming. Here's a brief overview of the content:

- **Chapters 1-6**: These chapters cover the basics of **C# syntax**, **variables**, **control structures**, and **functions**, as well as core OOP principles like **classes**, **objects**, **encapsulation**, and **constructors**.

- **Chapters 7-12**: Focus on more advanced concepts like **inheritance**, **polymorphism**, **abstract classes**, **interfaces**, **error handling**, and **collections**.

- **Chapters 13-17**: Explore advanced topics such as **delegates**, **events**, **LINQ**, **file I/O**, and **reflection**, all of which are critical for building flexible and high-performing applications.

- **Chapters 18-22**: These chapters take a deep dive into **attributes**, **dependency injection**, **unit testing**, **TDD**, and **design patterns**, all of which are essential for writing clean, maintainable, and testable code.

- **Chapters 23-26**: Bring everything together with practical lessons on building **real-world applications**, deploying software, and adhering to **best practices** in OOP.

*Why C#?*

C# is one of the most widely-used programming languages in the world, and for good reason. Developed by **Microsoft**, C# is part of the **.NET ecosystem**, which is one of the most powerful and flexible platforms for building modern applications. Whether you're building **web applications**, **desktop software**, **mobile apps**, or **games**, C# has the tools and libraries to support your development needs.

Some reasons to master C# and OOP:

- **Cross-platform development**: With the advent of .NET Core and .NET 5, C# can now run on **Windows**, **Linux**, and **macOS**.
- **Enterprise-grade applications**: C# is widely used in large-scale enterprise applications, thanks to its scalability, security features, and ease of integration with databases and other systems.
- **Rich ecosystem**: C# has a vast ecosystem of libraries, frameworks, and tools for everything from **data science** to **game development** with **Unity**.
- **Strong community support**: The C# community is active and continually growing, with vast resources available for learning, troubleshooting, and collaboration.

By mastering C# and OOP, you'll be well-equipped to develop applications that are not only functional but also clean, maintainable, and easily extendable.

*Mastering C# and OOP: The Path Forward*

This book is designed to take you from a beginner to an advanced C# developer. Whether you're new to C# or looking to deepen your understanding of object-oriented design principles, you will find the concepts and practices explained here to be invaluable in your development journey.

The skills you learn from this book will help you build high-quality software that is **modular**, **flexible**, and **scalable**, enabling you to take on real-world projects with confidence. From building small applications to large-scale systems, C# and OOP will serve as the foundation for your success.

So, let's get started! Whether you're coding your first C# project or refining your knowledge of OOP principles, this book will guide you every step of the way. Let's unlock the full power of **C#** and **Object-Oriented Programming** together!

If you're ready, turn the page, and let's dive into the exciting world of C# development!

# CHAPTER 1

# INTRODUCTION TO C# AND OBJECT-ORIENTED PROGRAMMING

Welcome to your first step in mastering C# and Object-Oriented Programming (OOP). In this chapter, we'll lay the foundation by introducing you to the C# language and OOP concepts. This will give you the background to understand the power of OOP and how it can improve your ability to write clean, reusable, and scalable code.

## Overview of C# as a Language

C# (pronounced "C-sharp") is a modern, versatile programming language developed by Microsoft as part of its .NET initiative. It's used for a wide range of applications, from desktop and web applications to games and mobile apps.

**Key Features of C#:**

- **Object-Oriented:** C# is built around the principles of OOP, which helps in organizing complex programs by modeling them around real-world objects.
- **Cross-Platform:** With .NET Core, C# applications can run on Windows, macOS, and Linux.
- **Rich Library Support:** C# has a robust set of libraries (e.g., .NET Framework, .NET Core) that make development faster and easier, including tools for web services, database connectivity, and user interfaces.
- **Type-Safety:** C# is a statically typed language, meaning the compiler catches many types of errors before your program runs.

C# is used by developers in various fields, from creating business applications to game development (using Unity), making it one of the most versatile languages in modern software development.

*Basics of Object-Oriented Programming (OOP)*

At the core of OOP lies the concept of **objects**. An object can be thought of as a collection of properties (data) and behaviors (functions or methods). OOP is based on four fundamental principles that help organize and structure code in a way that's easier to maintain, reuse, and extend.

Here's a breakdown of the main OOP concepts:

13

1. **Encapsulation:**

   Encapsulation refers to the concept of bundling data (variables) and the methods (functions) that operate on that data into a single unit or class. It also involves controlling access to the internal workings of the class via access modifiers like `public` and `private`. This helps to hide complexity and protect the integrity of the data.

   o **Example:** A bank account class could have private variables (balance, account number) and public methods (deposit, withdraw) to access or modify these values.

2. **Inheritance:**

   Inheritance allows one class (a "child") to inherit properties and methods from another class (a "parent"). This enables code reuse, which simplifies maintenance and reduces redundancy.

   o **Example:** A `Car` class might inherit from a `Vehicle` class. The `Vehicle` class has basic properties like `speed` and `fuel`, while `Car` adds specific properties like `engine type` and `model`.

3. **Polymorphism:**

   Polymorphism enables a single interface (method) to be used for different data types. This is typically achieved through **method overriding** or **method overloading**.

14

o **Example:** A `Draw()` method can be used for different shapes (circle, rectangle), where each shape defines its own version of how it should be drawn.

4. **Abstraction:**

   Abstraction involves hiding the complex implementation details of a class and exposing only the essential features. This makes it easier to interact with an object without needing to understand its internal workings.

   o **Example:** A TV remote hides the complexity of how the television works and provides a simple interface (buttons for power, volume, etc.).

---

*Real-World Analogy of OOP*

To make these OOP concepts clearer, let's use a real-world analogy. Imagine you're managing a **library system**:

- **Objects:** Each book, user, or librarian is an object in the system. Each of these objects has properties (e.g., a book has a title, author, and genre; a user has a name and a list of borrowed books).
- **Classes:** The blueprint for each type of object is a class. For example, you could have a `Book` class, a `User` class, and a `Librarian` class. These classes define the properties and behaviors of their respective objects.

- **Encapsulation:** A user object could have a private property for the number of books borrowed, and public methods to borrow or return books.

- **Inheritance:** You could have a class `Employee` that includes shared properties like `name` and `ID`. Then, classes `Librarian` and `Assistant` could inherit from `Employee`, each adding specific properties or methods.

- **Polymorphism:** A `Search()` method could behave differently based on the type of search (e.g., searching by book title, author, or genre).

- **Abstraction:** The library system's code for checking out a book might be abstracted into a simple method call like `CheckOutBook()`, even though the underlying code may involve checking availability, verifying user credentials, and updating records.

---

*Why OOP is Important in Modern Software Development*

OOP is widely used because it helps developers write clean, reusable, and maintainable code. Here are some key reasons why OOP is important:

1. **Code Reusability:** With inheritance and polymorphism, you can reuse code from existing classes and extend them with minimal changes, reducing redundancy and effort.

2. **Maintainability:** By organizing code into logical units (classes and objects), OOP makes it easier to manage large and complex codebases. Bugs can be isolated within specific objects or classes, making it easier to fix them.

3. **Scalability:** OOP makes it easier to extend applications by adding new classes without disturbing existing code. This is especially important in large projects that need to evolve over time.

4. **Modularity:** OOP encourages the use of smaller, independent modules (classes), which can be developed, tested, and maintained separately.

5. **Security and Flexibility:** Through encapsulation, OOP provides better control over data, ensuring that users can interact with data in a safe and secure manner. It also allows for better flexibility when modifying code or creating new features.

**Summary:** In this chapter, we've covered the basics of C# as a language and introduced the foundational principles of Object-Oriented Programming. You now understand how OOP structures code in a more manageable, reusable, and scalable way, with real-world analogies to help solidify these concepts. As we move forward in the book, we'll dive deeper into each of these principles, showing you how to apply them effectively using C#.

# CHAPTER 2

# SETTING UP YOUR C# DEVELOPMENT ENVIRONMENT

Now that you're familiar with the basics of C# and Object-Oriented Programming (OOP), it's time to set up your development environment. In this chapter, we will guide you through the process of installing the necessary tools and setting up a C# development environment on your system. By the end of this chapter, you'll be able to create and run your first C# project.

*Installing Visual Studio / Visual Studio Code*

To start coding in C#, you'll need an Integrated Development Environment (IDE) where you can write, debug, and compile your C# programs. Two popular options for C# development are **Visual Studio** and **Visual Studio Code**. Both are free, but they serve different purposes. Let's go over both options so you can choose the one that fits your needs.

Visual Studio

**Visual Studio** is a comprehensive, full-featured IDE for .NET development, including C#. It's suitable for building large applications and provides powerful debugging tools, IntelliSense (code completion), and much more.

1. **Download and Install Visual Studio:**
   - Visit the Visual Studio website.
   - Choose the **Community** edition (free for individual developers).
   - Run the installer after downloading.
   - During installation, you'll be prompted to select workloads. For C# development, select the **.NET desktop development** and **ASP.NET and web development** workloads (you can always add more workloads later).
   - Click "Install" and wait for the process to complete.

2. **Launching Visual Studio:**
   - After installation, open Visual Studio.
   - You may be prompted to sign in with a Microsoft account (optional).
   - You're now ready to start creating C# projects!

Visual Studio Code

**Visual Studio Code (VS Code)** is a lightweight, cross-platform editor for coding, and while it's not as feature-rich as Visual Studio, it's perfect for smaller projects, web applications, or if you prefer a more minimalist environment.

1. **Download and Install Visual Studio Code:**
   o Visit the Visual Studio Code website.
   o Download and install the version for your operating system (Windows, macOS, or Linux).
   o After installation, launch VS Code.

2. **Install the C# Extension:**
   o Open VS Code, and go to the Extensions view by clicking on the Extensions icon in the Activity Bar on the side of the window.
   o Search for the **C#** extension and install it. This extension is provided by Microsoft and will give you syntax highlighting, IntelliSense, and debugging support for C#.
   o Additionally, you might want to install **.NET Core SDK** if you plan on building .NET Core applications.

3. **Setting Up the .NET SDK:**
   o To ensure everything is working correctly, download the **.NET SDK** from the official Microsoft website.

    o   The SDK includes everything you need to run, build, and deploy .NET applications, including C# projects.

---

*Introduction to .NET Framework and .NET Core*

Now that you have your editor set up, it's essential to understand the two main frameworks used for building C# applications: **.NET Framework** and **.NET Core**.

---

.NET Framework

The **.NET Framework** is the original, Windows-only framework for building .NET applications. It's used primarily for Windows desktop applications and web applications running on IIS (Internet Information Services). Although it's still widely used, Microsoft has shifted much of its focus to .NET Core for new projects due to its flexibility and cross-platform capabilities.

- **Use Case:** If you're building desktop applications or legacy applications for Windows, you'll typically use the .NET Framework.
- **Platform:** Windows only.

.NET Core

**.NET Core** is a more modern, cross-platform framework that allows you to build applications that run on Windows, macOS, and Linux. It's the recommended framework for most new projects because it supports cloud-based applications, microservices, web APIs, and much more.

- **Use Case:** Ideal for building web applications, microservices, and console apps. It's also great for projects that need to run on multiple platforms.
- **Platform:** Cross-platform (Windows, macOS, and Linux).

---

.NET 5 and Beyond

With the release of **.NET 5**, Microsoft has unified .NET Framework and .NET Core into a single platform. This means that .NET Core has evolved into the unified **.NET 5**, and future versions (like .NET 6 and .NET 7) will continue to build on this platform. When you start a new project, it's recommended to use .NET 5 or later.

*Creating Your First C# Project*

Now that you've installed Visual Studio or Visual Studio Code and understand the difference between .NET Framework and .NET Core, let's create your first C# project.

Creating a Console Application in Visual Studio

1. **Open Visual Studio.**
2. **Create a New Project:**
   - Click on "Create a new project."
   - Choose **Console App** (for a simple text-based application).
   - Select **C#** and **.NET 5 (or higher)** as the framework.
   - Name your project (e.g., `HelloWorld`), choose a location, and click "Create."
3. **Write Your First Program:**
   - Visual Studio will create a simple template for you. You'll see a `Program.cs` file.
   - Replace the `Main` method with the following code to print a message to the console:

```csharp
using System;
```

```
class Program
{
    static void Main()
    {
        Console.WriteLine("Hello,
World!");
    }
}
```

4. **Run the Program:**

   o Press **F5** or click the "Start" button to run the program.

   o You should see "Hello, World!" printed to the console.

---

Creating a Console Application in Visual Studio Code

1. **Open Visual Studio Code.**

2. **Open the Terminal:**

   o Go to the **Terminal** menu and select **New Terminal**.

3. **Create a New Project:**

   o In the terminal, navigate to the folder where you want to create your project.

   o Type the following command to create a new console application:

```bash
bash
```

```bash
dotnet new console -n HelloWorld
```

4. **Navigate to the Project Folder:**
   o Change to the project directory:

```bash
bash
```

```bash
cd HelloWorld
```

5. **Write Your First Program:**
   o Open the `Program.cs` file and replace its content with the same code as before:

```csharp
csharp

using System;

class Program
{
    static void Main()
    {
        Console.WriteLine("Hello,
World!");
    }
}
```

6. **Run the Program:**
   o In the terminal, run the following command:

```bash
```

```
dotnet run
```

- o You should see "Hello, World!" printed to the terminal.

---

*Conclusion*

In this chapter, you've learned how to install and configure your C# development environment using either Visual Studio or Visual Studio Code. You also learned about .NET Framework and .NET Core (and the unification in .NET 5), and you created your first simple C# console application.

With your environment set up and your first project running, you're ready to dive deeper into C# programming and explore more advanced topics in the coming chapters.

# CHAPTER 3

# BASIC SYNTAX AND STRUCTURE OF C#

In this chapter, we'll dive into the essential components of C# syntax and structure. You'll learn about variables, data types, operators, control flow, and how to write functions and methods. These are the building blocks that every C# developer needs to understand in order to write meaningful and efficient code.

## Variables, Data Types, and Operators

Before you start coding, it's crucial to understand how to store and manipulate data. In C#, this is done using **variables** and **data types**.

## Variables

A **variable** is a container for storing data. Each variable in C# has a specific **data type** that determines what kind of data it can hold. When declaring a variable, you must specify its data type and give it a name.

```
csharp

int age;   // Declaration of an integer variable
named 'age'
age = 25; // Assigning a value of 25 to the 'age'
variable
```

Alternatively, you can declare and initialize a variable in a single statement:

```
csharp

int age = 25;   // Declaration and initialization
in one line
```

Data Types

In C#, there are various **primitive data types** that allow you to store different kinds of data. Here are the most commonly used ones:

- **int**: Stores integer numbers (whole numbers) like `-2`, `0`, `42`.
- **double**: Stores floating-point numbers (decimal numbers) like `3.14`, `0.001`, `-7.2`.
- **bool**: Stores Boolean values, `true` or `false`.
- **char**: Stores a single character, like `'A'`, `'b'`, or `'3'`.

- **string**: Stores a sequence of characters, like `"Hello, World!"`.
- **decimal**: Similar to `double`, but more precise. Typically used for financial calculations.
- **var**: A keyword that allows the compiler to infer the data type of the variable based on the value you assign.

Example:

csharp

```
int number = 10;
double price = 99.99;
bool isActive = true;
char grade = 'A';
string message = "Hello, C#!";
```

Operators

Operators are symbols used to perform operations on variables or values. Some common categories of operators include:

- **Arithmetic Operators:** Used for basic mathematical operations.
    - + (addition)
    - - (subtraction)
    - * (multiplication)

29

- o  / (division)
- o  % (modulus, or remainder)

Example:

csharp

```
int result = 10 + 5;   // result = 15
int quotient = 10 / 2;   // quotient = 5
```

- **Comparison Operators:** Used to compare two values and return a boolean value.
  - o  == (equal to)
  - o  != (not equal to)
  - o  > (greater than)
  - o  < (less than)
  - o  >= (greater than or equal to)
  - o  <= (less than or equal to)

Example:

csharp

```
bool isEqual = 10 == 5;   // isEqual = false
bool isGreater = 10 > 5;   // isGreater =
true
```

- **Logical Operators:** Used to combine multiple conditions.

30

- &&  (AND)
- ||  (OR)
- !  (NOT)

Example:

csharp

```
bool result = (5 > 3) && (7 < 10);   //
result = true
```

---

*Control Flow: if, switch, and loops*

Control flow structures allow you to make decisions and repeat actions in your program. C# provides several control flow mechanisms, including conditional statements and loops.

---

if Statement

The `if` statement is used to execute a block of code only if a certain condition is true.

csharp

```
int age = 18;

if (age >= 18)
```

```csharp
{
    Console.WriteLine("You are an adult.");
}
else
{
    Console.WriteLine("You are a minor.");
}
```

You can also use `else if` to check multiple conditions:

csharp

```csharp
int number = 10;

if (number > 10)
{
    Console.WriteLine("Number is greater than 10.");
}
else if (number < 10)
{
    Console.WriteLine("Number is less than 10.");
}
else
{
    Console.WriteLine("Number is equal to 10.");
}
```

switch Statement

The switch statement is another way to make decisions. It's more efficient when you have multiple possible values to check for a single variable.

```csharp
int dayOfWeek = 3;

switch (dayOfWeek)
{
    case 1:
        Console.WriteLine("Monday");
        break;
    case 2:
        Console.WriteLine("Tuesday");
        break;
    case 3:
        Console.WriteLine("Wednesday");
        break;
    default:
        Console.WriteLine("Unknown day");
        break;
}
```

The break keyword is used to exit the switch statement once a case has been matched.

## Loops

Loops allow you to repeat a block of code multiple times.

- **for loop**: Best used when you know how many times you want to repeat a block of code.

  csharp

  ```csharp
  for (int i = 0; i < 5; i++)
  {
      Console.WriteLine(i); // Prints 0 to 4
  }
  ```

- **while loop**: Repeats a block of code while a condition is true.

  csharp

  ```csharp
  int i = 0;
  while (i < 5)
  {
      Console.WriteLine(i); // Prints 0 to 4
      i++;
  }
  ```

- **do-while loop**: Similar to the while loop, but guarantees that the block of code will be executed at least once.

```
csharp

int i = 0;
do
{
    Console.WriteLine(i); // Prints 0 to 4
    i++;
}
while (i < 5);
```

## Functions and Methods

A **function** (or **method**) is a block of code that performs a specific task. Functions are fundamental to organizing your program into manageable chunks and improving code reusability.

## Creating a Method

In C#, a method is defined within a class and is typically called in response to some action (like a button click or a loop iteration).

```
csharp

class Program
{
    static void Main()
    {
```

35

```
        // Calling the method
        SayHello("Alice");
    }

    // Method definition
    static void SayHello(string name)
    {
        Console.WriteLine("Hello,  " + name +
"!");
    }
}
```

In this example, the SayHello method takes one parameter (name) and prints a greeting message.

---

Method Return Types

Methods can return values. The return type is specified before the method name. For example, if you want a method to return an integer, you would define it like this:

csharp

```
static int AddNumbers(int a, int b)
{
    return a + b;
}
```

```
int result = AddNumbers(3, 4);  // result = 7
Console.WriteLine(result);
```

In this case, the `AddNumbers` method takes two integers as parameters and returns their sum.

---

## Method Overloading

C# allows you to create multiple methods with the same name, as long as their parameter lists are different. This is known as **method overloading**.

csharp

```
class Program
{
    static void Main()
    {
        Console.WriteLine(AddNumbers(2,    3));
// Calls AddNumbers(int, int)
        Console.WriteLine(AddNumbers(2.5, 3.5));
// Calls AddNumbers(double, double)
    }

    static int AddNumbers(int a, int b)    //
Integer version
    {
        return a + b;
```

```
    }


    static double AddNumbers(double a, double b)
// Double version
    {
        return a + b;
    }
}
```

---

*Conclusion*

In this chapter, you've learned the basics of C# syntax and structure. We covered how to declare variables, work with different data types, and use operators. We also explored control flow mechanisms like `if`, `switch`, and loops, which allow you to make decisions and repeat actions. Finally, we introduced you to functions and methods—how to define them, call them, and return values from them.

With this knowledge, you're ready to start writing simple, but meaningful, programs. In the next chapters, we'll build on these concepts and explore more advanced features of C#. If you need clarification or want to dive deeper into any of the topics covered here, let me know!

# *CHAPTER 4*

# *UNDERSTANDING CLASSES AND OBJECTS*

In this chapter, we will explore one of the fundamental concepts of Object-Oriented Programming (OOP)—**classes** and **objects**. Understanding how to create and work with classes and objects is crucial for mastering C#. We'll break down the concept with simple explanations, followed by a real-world example to help you understand how these concepts fit together.

*What is a Class?*

A **class** is a blueprint or template for creating objects. It defines the properties (data) and behaviors (methods) that the objects created from it will have. You can think of a class as a **cookie cutter**, and the objects are the **cookies** that are shaped according to the class.

A class doesn't actually hold any data until you create an object (an instance) from it. The class defines how objects will behave and what information they will store, but the objects hold the actual data.

39

Here's a simple analogy:

- **Class**: A blueprint for a house (defines the number of rooms, doors, windows, etc.)
- **Object**: A specific house built from that blueprint (actual physical house with specific features like colors, furniture, and size).

---

### What is an Object?

An **object** is an instance of a class. It's a specific realization of the class, created using the blueprint provided by the class. Once an object is created, it can hold actual data in its properties and execute the methods defined by the class.

Using the house analogy again:

- **Object**: A specific house that is built using the blueprint. This house can have its own specific values for attributes such as color, size, and number of rooms.

---

### Creating Classes and Objects in C#

Now that we understand what classes and objects are, let's see how we create them in C#.

Creating a Class in C#

To define a class in C#, you use the `class` keyword, followed by the name of the class. Within the class, you define **fields**, **properties**, and **methods**.

Here's an example of a basic `Car` class:

```csharp

class Car
{
    // Fields
    public string make;
    public string model;
    public int year;
    public double speed;

    // Method (behavior of the Car)
    public void Accelerate()
    {
        speed += 10;  // Increase speed by 10
        Console.WriteLine("The car accelerates. Current speed: " + speed + " mph.");
    }

    public void Brake()
    {
        speed -= 10;  // Decrease speed by 10
```

```
        Console.WriteLine("The   car   slows   down.
Current  speed:  "  +  speed  +  "  mph.");
    }
}
```

In this example:

- **Fields** like make, model, year, and speed store the data related to the Car.
- **Methods** like Accelerate() and Brake() define the actions or behaviors that the Car can perform.

### Creating an Object from a Class

Once you've defined a class, you can create **objects** (instances) of that class using the new keyword. An object is created by calling the constructor of the class, which initializes the object's fields and sets them to their default or provided values.

Here's how to create an object from the Car class:

csharp

```csharp
class Program
{
    static void Main()
    {
        // Creating an object of the Car class
        Car myCar = new Car();
```

```
    // Setting values for the object
    myCar.make = "Toyota";
    myCar.model = "Camry";
    myCar.year = 2022;
    myCar.speed = 0;

    // Using methods of the object
    Console.WriteLine("Car    Details:    "    +
myCar.make   +   "   "   +   myCar.model   +   "   "   +
myCar.year);
    myCar.Accelerate();
    myCar.Brake();
  }
}
```

## Breakdown of the code:

- `Car myCar = new Car();`: This creates a new object of the `Car` class called `myCar`.
- `myCar.make = "Toyota";`: This sets the `make` field of the `myCar` object to `"Toyota"`.
- `myCar.Accelerate();`: This calls the `Accelerate()` method of the `myCar` object, which increases its speed by 10.

When you run the program, the output will be:

```
yaml
```

```
Car Details: Toyota Camry 2022
The car accelerates. Current speed: 10 mph.
The car slows down. Current speed: 0 mph.
```

---

*Real-World Example: "Car" Class*

Let's extend our `Car` class with more real-world features to better illustrate how classes and objects work in C#.

Imagine you want to simulate the behavior of several cars, each with different makes, models, and behaviors. You can create objects for different cars, each with unique data.

Here's an enhanced version of the `Car` class:

csharp

```csharp
class Car
{
    // Fields
    public string make;
    public string model;
    public int year;
    public double speed;
    public string color;

    // Constructor to initialize a new Car object
```

```csharp
    public Car(string carMake, string carModel,
int carYear, string carColor)
    {
        make = carMake;
        model = carModel;
        year = carYear;
        color = carColor;
        speed = 0; // Cars start with a speed of
0
    }

    // Method to accelerate the car
    public void Accelerate()
    {
        speed += 10;
        Console.WriteLine($"The {make} {model}
accelerates. Current speed: {speed} mph.");
    }

    // Method to brake the car
    public void Brake()
    {
        speed -= 10;
        Console.WriteLine($"The {make} {model}
slows down. Current speed: {speed} mph.");
    }

    // Method to display car details
    public void DisplayDetails()
```

45

```
    {
        Console.WriteLine($"Car: {make} {model},
Year: {year}, Color: {color}");
    }
}
```

In this version:

- **Constructor**: The Car class has a constructor that allows you to initialize the fields (make, model, year, and color) when you create a new object.
- **DisplayDetails()**: This method is used to print the car's details.

Creating Multiple Car Objects

Now, let's create multiple Car objects with different values:

csharp

```
class Program
{
    static void Main()
    {
        // Creating objects for different cars
        Car car1 = new Car("Toyota", "Corolla",
2021, "Red");
```

```csharp
        Car  car2  =  new  Car("Honda",  "Civic",
2022, "Blue");

        // Displaying details of the cars
        car1.DisplayDetails();
        car2.DisplayDetails();

        // Using methods on the car objects
        car1.Accelerate();
        car2.Accelerate();
        car1.Brake();
    }
}
```

When you run the program, the output will be:

yaml

```
Car: Toyota Corolla, Year: 2021, Color: Red
Car: Honda Civic, Year: 2022, Color: Blue
The Toyota Corolla accelerates. Current speed: 10
mph.
The Honda Civic accelerates. Current speed: 10
mph.
The Toyota Corolla slows down. Current speed: 0
mph.
```

*Summary*

In this chapter, you've learned the basics of **classes** and **objects** in C#. You now know that:

- A **class** is a blueprint that defines the properties and behaviors of objects.
- An **object** is an instance of a class, created using the `new` keyword.
- You can define fields, methods, and even constructors to initialize objects when they're created.

By using classes and objects, you can model real-world entities and their behaviors in a structured and efficient way. This is the core of Object-Oriented Programming.

Let me know if you'd like to explore any of these concepts further or if you're ready to move on to the next chapter!

# CHAPTER 5

# ENCAPSULATION: PROTECTING DATA

In Object-Oriented Programming (OOP), **encapsulation** is a fundamental concept that helps us organize and protect the data within objects. Encapsulation refers to bundling data (variables) and the methods that operate on that data into a single unit or class and restricting access to certain parts of that data. This is done by using **access modifiers**, which control how data is accessed and modified. The goal is to ensure that data is not exposed or modified inappropriately, maintaining the integrity of the object.

In this chapter, we'll explore how encapsulation works in C# using **access modifiers**, the difference between **properties** and **fields**, and how to apply encapsulation with a real-world example—a **bank account** class.

---

*Access Modifiers: Controlling Access to Data*

In C#, **access modifiers** define the scope and visibility of classes, fields, methods, and properties. The most commonly used access modifiers are:

- **public**: This means that the member (field, method, property, etc.) is accessible from anywhere. It can be accessed both inside and outside the class.

- **private**: This restricts access to the member, meaning it can only be accessed within the class where it is declared. It is the default access modifier for class members if none is specified.

- **protected**: This allows access to the member within the class and any derived (subclass) classes.

- **internal**: This means that the member is accessible only within the same assembly (project) but not from outside the project.

- **protected internal**: This allows access to the member from both the current assembly and derived classes.

- **private protected**: This means that the member is accessible only within the current class and derived classes within the same assembly.

Let's look at an example to understand these better:

```csharp

class Account
{
    public string accountHolderName;   // Can be accessed from anywhere
```

```csharp
    private double balance;    // Can only be
accessed within this class

    public    Account(string    name,    double
initialBalance)
    {
        accountHolderName = name;
        balance = initialBalance;
    }

    // Public method to get the balance
    public double GetBalance()
    {
        return balance;
    }

    // Public method to deposit money
    public void Deposit(double amount)
    {
        if (amount > 0)
        {
            balance += amount;
            Console.WriteLine($"{amount}
deposited. New balance: {balance}");
        }
        else
        {
            Console.WriteLine("Amount    must    be
positive.");
```

51

```
        }
    }
}
```

Here:

- `accountHolderName` is **public**, so it can be accessed directly from outside the class.
- `balance` is **private**, meaning it cannot be accessed directly outside the `Account` class.
- `GetBalance()` and `Deposit()` are **public methods**, allowing controlled access to the `balance` field. The method `Deposit` also includes validation to ensure the deposited amount is positive, protecting the `balance` from invalid changes.

---

*Properties vs. Fields*

In C#, there is an important distinction between **fields** and **properties**.

- **Field**: A field is a variable that holds data. Fields can have access modifiers (`public`, `private`, etc.) that control access to the data.
- **Property**: A property is a member of a class that provides access to a field. Properties can be used to **encapsulate** fields by controlling how they are accessed and modified.

A property usually has a **getter** (to read the value) and a **setter** (to modify the value). By using properties, you can add logic to validate data before it's set or retrieved, which provides a layer of control over how fields are accessed.

Here's an example of a **property** with a **getter** and **setter**:

csharp

```
class Account
{
    private double balance;  // private field

    // Property to control access to the balance
field
    public double Balance
    {
        get { return balance; }  // Getter
        set
        {
            if (value >= 0)    // Setter with
validation
            {
                balance = value;
            }
            else
            {
                Console.WriteLine("Balance
cannot be negative.");
```

53

```
        }
    }
}

public Account(double initialBalance)
{
    Balance = initialBalance;   // Using the
property to set the balance
}
}
```

In this case, `Balance` is a property that provides controlled access to the `balance` field. The **getter** simply returns the value of `balance`, while the **setter** ensures that the balance can never be set to a negative value. This approach is more flexible and safer than directly using a field.

---

*Real-World Example: A Bank Account Class with Encapsulation*

Let's put everything together with a more complete example—a `BankAccount` class that uses encapsulation to protect the balance and allow controlled access to it.

csharp

```
class BankAccount
{
    private string accountNumber;
```

```csharp
    private string accountHolder;
    private double balance;

    // Constructor to initialize the bank account
    public  BankAccount(string  accountNumber,
string accountHolder, double initialBalance)
    {
        this.accountNumber = accountNumber;
        this.accountHolder = accountHolder;
        this.balance = initialBalance;
    }

    // Public property to access the balance
    public double Balance
    {
        get { return balance; }
        private set
        {
            if (value < 0)
                Console.WriteLine("Error:
Balance cannot be negative.");
            else
                balance = value;
        }
    }

    // Method to deposit money
    public void Deposit(double amount)
    {
```

```csharp
        if (amount > 0)
        {
            Balance += amount;   // Using the
property to set balance
            Console.WriteLine($"{amount}
deposited. New balance: {Balance}");
        }
        else
        {
            Console.WriteLine("Error:    Deposit
amount must be positive.");
        }
    }

    // Method to withdraw money
    public void Withdraw(double amount)
    {
        if (amount > 0 && amount <= Balance)
        {
            Balance -= amount;   // Using the
property to set balance
            Console.WriteLine($"{amount}
withdrawn. New balance: {Balance}");
        }
        else if (amount <= 0)
        {
            Console.WriteLine("Error: Withdrawal
amount must be positive.");
        }
```

```
        else
        {
            Console.WriteLine("Error:
Insufficient funds.");
        }
    }


    // Method to display account details
    public void DisplayAccountDetails()
    {
        Console.WriteLine($"Account       Number:
{accountNumber}\nAccount             Holder:
{accountHolder}\nBalance: {Balance}");
    }
}
```

## Using the BankAccount Class

Here's how you can create and use the BankAccount class:

csharp

```
class Program
{
    static void Main()
    {
        // Create a new bank account with an
initial balance
```

```
        BankAccount      account      =      new
BankAccount("123456", "John Doe", 1000.00);

        // Display account details
        account.DisplayAccountDetails();

        // Deposit money
        account.Deposit(500);

        // Withdraw money
        account.Withdraw(200);

        // Try to withdraw more than the balance
        account.Withdraw(1500);
    }
}
```

The output will be:

```
yaml

Account Number: 123456
Account Holder: John Doe
Balance: 1000
500 deposited. New balance: 1500
200 withdrawn. New balance: 1300
Error: Insufficient funds.
```

In this example:

- The `balance` field is encapsulated by a property `Balance`, which controls access to it.
- The `Deposit` and `Withdraw` methods are public and allow controlled modifications to the `balance`.
- The `Withdraw` method checks for valid amounts and prevents withdrawals that would cause the balance to go negative.
- The `accountNumber` and `accountHolder` fields are private, ensuring that sensitive information cannot be changed directly.

---

*Summary*

In this chapter, we learned about **encapsulation**, which is a powerful way to protect data within an object. By using **access modifiers**, we control how and where the data can be accessed or modified. **Properties** provide a controlled way to access fields and can include logic to ensure data integrity.

We applied these concepts to a real-world example—a `BankAccount` class—where we encapsulated the balance and provided controlled access to it through public methods and properties. This ensures that the bank account data is protected and the object behaves as expected.

Let me know if you want to dive deeper into any of these concepts or if you're ready to move on to the next chapter!

# *CHAPTER 6*

# *CONSTRUCTORS AND DESTRUCTORS*

In this chapter, we will explore two important features of C# that help manage the lifecycle of objects: **constructors** and **destructors**. These features ensure that objects are properly initialized when they are created and cleaned up when they are no longer needed. We'll also look at **constructor overloading**, which allows you to define multiple constructors with different parameters, and the **destructor (finalizer)**, which is used to perform cleanup tasks before an object is destroyed.

---

*What is a Constructor?*

A **constructor** is a special method that is called automatically when an object of a class is created. It is used to initialize the object's state—i.e., to assign initial values to the fields or properties of the object. Constructors allow you to set up objects with meaningful initial data when they are created.

In C#, a constructor has the following characteristics:

- It has the **same name as the class**.

- It does **not have a return type** (not even `void`).
- It is automatically called when an object is instantiated (created) using the `new` keyword.

Here's an example of a simple constructor:

csharp

```csharp
class User
{
    public string name;
    public int age;

    // Constructor to initialize the User object
    public User(string userName, int userAge)
    {
        name = userName;
        age = userAge;
        Console.WriteLine("User  created:  "  +
name + ", Age: " + age);
    }
}
```

In this example:

- The constructor `User(string userName, int userAge)` initializes the `name` and `age` properties when a `User` object is created.

Creating an Object Using a Constructor

csharp

```csharp
class Program
{
    static void Main()
    {
        // Creating a new User object using the
constructor
        User user1 = new User("Alice", 30);
        User user2 = new User("Bob", 25);
    }
}
```

When you run this program, the output will be:

yaml

```yaml
User created: Alice, Age: 30
User created: Bob, Age: 25
```

Each time a `User` object is created, the constructor is automatically called to initialize the object.

---

*Constructor Overloading*

**Constructor overloading** occurs when a class has more than one constructor with the same name, but different parameters. This

63

allows you to create objects in multiple ways by providing different sets of initial values. Each constructor can have a different number or type of parameters.

Here's an example of constructor overloading:

```csharp
class User
{
    public string name;
    public int age;

    // Constructor with two parameters
    public User(string userName, int userAge)
    {
        name = userName;
        age = userAge;
    }

    // Constructor with one parameter (overloaded
constructor)
    public User(string userName)
    {
        name = userName;
        age = 0;  // Default age
    }
```

```csharp
    // Constructor with no parameters (overloaded
constructor)
    public User()
    {
        name = "Unknown";
        age = 0;
    }
}
```

In this example:

- The first constructor takes two parameters: `userName` and `userAge`.
- The second constructor takes only one parameter: `userName`, and it sets a default value of `0` for `age`.
- The third constructor has no parameters and provides default values for both `name` and `age`.

Creating Objects Using Different Constructors
csharp

```csharp
class Program
{
    static void Main()
    {
        // Using the constructor with two
parameters
        User user1 = new User("Alice", 30);
```

```
        // Using the constructor with one
parameter
        User user2 = new User("Bob");

        // Using the constructor with no
parameters
        User user3 = new User();
    }
}
```

The output will be:

```
yaml


User created: Alice, Age: 30
User created: Bob, Age: 0
User created: Unknown, Age: 0
```

Constructor overloading is useful when you want to provide different ways to initialize objects depending on the situation.

_____

*Destructor (Finalizer) in C#*

A **destructor** (also called a **finalizer**) is a special method that is used to perform cleanup operations before an object is destroyed. It is automatically called when an object is garbage collected (when it is no longer needed and the memory is reclaimed by the .NET runtime).

In C#, destructors are defined using the ~ symbol followed by the class name. However, it is important to note that destructors are not as commonly used in C# as in other languages because C# has automatic garbage collection, which takes care of memory management for you.

The destructor is typically used for releasing unmanaged resources like file handles, network connections, or database connections. It is not recommended to rely heavily on destructors, as the garbage collector's timing is not predictable.

Here's an example of a destructor:

```csharp
class User
{
    public string name;

    // Constructor to initialize the User object
    public User(string userName)
    {
        name = userName;
        Console.WriteLine(name + " created.");
    }

    // Destructor (finalizer)
    ~User()
    {
```

```
        // Perform cleanup tasks before object is
destroyed
        Console.WriteLine(name + " is being
destroyed.");
    }
}
```

In this example:

- The User class has a constructor to initialize the name.
- The destructor ~User() will be called automatically when the object is about to be destroyed. It is used to perform any necessary cleanup tasks.

Creating and Destroying Objects

csharp

```
class Program
{
    static void Main()
    {
        // Creating a User object
        User user1 = new User("Alice");

        // Explicitly forcing garbage collection
for demonstration
        GC.Collect();
        GC.WaitForPendingFinalizers();
    }
```

}

When you run the program, you may see the following output:

```
csharp
```

```
Alice created.
Alice is being destroyed.
```

Note: The destructor will be called when the garbage collector decides to clean up the object. The explicit garbage collection (`GC.Collect()`) is used here just to demonstrate the destructor. In real-world scenarios, the garbage collector manages object cleanup automatically.

*Real-World Example: Initialization and Cleanup in a "User" Class*

Let's apply constructors and destructors in a more realistic example of a `User` class that might represent a user in an application. In this case, we'll assume that the `User` class uses a database connection, which needs to be opened during initialization and closed during cleanup.

```
csharp
```

```
class User
{
    private string name;
```

69

```csharp
    private string email;
    private bool databaseConnectionOpen;

    // Constructor to initialize the User object
and open a database connection
    public    User(string    userName,    string
userEmail)
    {
        name = userName;
        email = userEmail;
        OpenDatabaseConnection();
    }

    // Method  to  simulate  opening  a  database
connection
    private void OpenDatabaseConnection()
    {
        databaseConnectionOpen = true;
        Console.WriteLine("Database    connection
opened for user: " + name);
    }

    //  Destructor  to  close  the  database
connection before the object is destroyed
    ~User()
    {
        if (databaseConnectionOpen)
        {
            CloseDatabaseConnection();
```

```
        }
    }

    // Method to close the database connection
    private void CloseDatabaseConnection()
    {
        databaseConnectionOpen = false;
        Console.WriteLine("Database     connection
closed for user: " + name);
    }

    // Method to display user details
    public void DisplayDetails()
    {
        Console.WriteLine("Name:     "   +   name   +
"\nEmail: " + email);
    }
}
```

In this example:

- The constructor initializes the User object and opens a
  simulated database connection using the
  OpenDatabaseConnection() method.
- The destructor ensures that if the User object is
  destroyed, the database connection is properly closed by
  calling CloseDatabaseConnection().

Using the User Class

csharp

```
class Program
{
    static void Main()
    {
        // Creating a User object
        User    user1   =    new    User("Alice",
"alice@example.com");

        // Displaying user details
        user1.DisplayDetails();

        // Explicitly forcing garbage collection
for demonstration
        GC.Collect();
        GC.WaitForPendingFinalizers();
    }
}
```

The output will be:

pgsql

```
Database connection opened for user: Alice
Name: Alice
Email: alice@example.com
Database connection closed for user: Alice
```

*Summary*

In this chapter, we learned about **constructors** and **destructors** in C#:

- **Constructors** are special methods used to initialize an object's state when it is created. They can be overloaded to provide different ways of initializing objects.
- **Destructors (finalizers)** are special methods that are called automatically when an object is about to be destroyed. They are useful for cleaning up unmanaged resources, though they are less commonly used due to automatic garbage collection in C#.

We also explored a real-world example where constructors and destructors are used to manage a database connection for a `User` class.

Let me know if you'd like to dive deeper into any of these concepts or continue to the next chapter!

# CHAPTER 7

# INHERITANCE: REUSING CODE

In this chapter, we'll dive into one of the most powerful concepts in Object-Oriented Programming (OOP)—**inheritance**. Inheritance allows a class to **inherit** the properties and methods of another class, enabling code reuse and making it easier to manage and extend code. We'll also explore how to create **base** and **derived** classes in C#, and finish with a real-world example using an **Animal class hierarchy**.

---

*What is Inheritance?*

**Inheritance** is a fundamental OOP concept where one class (called the **derived class**) inherits the properties and behaviors (methods) of another class (called the **base class**). This allows the derived class to reuse and extend the functionality provided by the base class, which helps avoid code duplication.

Inheritance provides two key benefits:

1. **Code Reusability**: You can write code once in a base class and reuse it in any derived class.

2. **Extensibility**: Derived classes can add their own unique behavior or override the behavior inherited from the base class.

Here's an analogy:

- **Base Class**: Think of it as a **general blueprint** (e.g., a general "Vehicle" class).
- **Derived Class**: It is a more **specific blueprint** that extends the general blueprint with additional details (e.g., a "Car" class or "Truck" class that inherits from the "Vehicle" class).

*Basic Inheritance in C#*

In C#, inheritance is achieved using the :, or **colon** symbol. When a class inherits from another class, it can access all **public** and **protected** members of the base class.

Here's a simple example of inheritance:

```csharp

class Animal
{
    // Properties of the Animal class
    public string name;
```

```csharp
    public int age;

    // Method of the Animal class
    public void Speak()
    {
        Console.WriteLine("The  animal  makes  a
sound.");
    }
}


// Derived class "Dog" that inherits from the
"Animal" base class
class Dog : Animal
{
    // Additional property specific to the Dog
class
    public string breed;

    // Overriding the Speak method to make a
specific sound
    public void Speak()
    {
        Console.WriteLine("The dog barks.");
    }
}
```

In this example:

- The **Animal** class is the **base class**, containing basic properties (`name` and `age`) and a method `Speak()`.
- The **Dog** class is a **derived class** that inherits from the **Animal** class and **overrides** the `Speak()` method to make a specific sound.

*Creating Base and Derived Classes*

To create base and derived classes in C#, follow these steps:

1. **Base class**: Define the class that will be inherited from. This class will contain common properties and methods.
2. **Derived class**: Use the `: baseClassName` syntax to inherit from the base class. The derived class can either use the inherited methods and properties as is or **override** them to provide its own implementation.

Here's an example demonstrating base and derived classes:

csharp

```csharp
class Animal
{
    public string name;
    public int age;
```

```csharp
    // Constructor to initialize the Animal
object
    public    Animal(string    animalName,    int
animalAge)
    {
        name = animalName;
        age = animalAge;
    }

    public virtual void Speak()  // Using virtual
to allow overriding
    {
        Console.WriteLine("The   animal   makes   a
sound.");
    }
}

// Derived class "Dog" inherits from "Animal"
class Dog : Animal
{
    public string breed;

    // Constructor to initialize Dog object
    public Dog(string dogName, int dogAge, string
dogBreed) : base(dogName, dogAge)
    {
        breed = dogBreed;
    }
```

```csharp
// Overriding the Speak method for the Dog
class
    public override void Speak()
    {
        Console.WriteLine($"The    {breed}    dog
barks.");
    }
}
```

- **Base class `Animal`** has a constructor that initializes the name and age properties and a `Speak()` method.
- **Derived class `Dog`** uses the : `base(dogName, dogAge)` syntax to call the base class constructor. It also **overrides** the `Speak()` method to give a specific behavior for the dog.

Creating Objects of Base and Derived Classes
csharp

```csharp
class Program
{
    static void Main()
    {
        // Create an object of the Dog class
        Dog dog1 = new Dog("Buddy", 3, "Golden
Retriever");

        // Access properties and methods from the
Dog object
```

```
        Console.WriteLine($"Dog          Name:
{dog1.name},     Age:     {dog1.age},      Breed:
{dog1.breed}");
        dog1.Speak();  // Calling the overridden
method
    }
}
```

The output will be:

yaml

```
Dog Name: Buddy, Age: 3, Breed: Golden Retriever
The Golden Retriever dog barks.
```

Here, we see that the Dog object is able to inherit the properties
name and age from the Animal class and also provide its own
Speak() method.

---

*Real-World Example: Animal Class Hierarchy*

Let's build a real-world example using inheritance to represent an
**Animal** class hierarchy. We will have a base class called Animal,
and several derived classes like Dog, Cat, and Bird, each
representing different animals that inherit from the Animal class.

csharp

```csharp
class Animal
{
    public string name;
    public int age;

    // Constructor for the Animal class
    public  Animal(string  animalName,  int
animalAge)
    {
        name = animalName;
        age = animalAge;
    }

    // Virtual method to be overridden in derived
classes
    public virtual void Speak()
    {
        Console.WriteLine("The  animal  makes  a
sound.");
    }
}

class Dog : Animal
{
    public string breed;

    // Constructor for the Dog class
    public Dog(string dogName, int dogAge, string
dogBreed) : base(dogName, dogAge)
```

```
    {
        breed = dogBreed;
    }

    public override void Speak()
    {
        Console.WriteLine($"The    {breed}    dog
barks.");
    }
}

class Cat : Animal
{
    public string color;

    // Constructor for the Cat class
    public Cat(string catName, int catAge, string
catColor) : base(catName, catAge)
    {
        color = catColor;
    }

    public override void Speak()
    {
        Console.WriteLine("The cat meows.");
    }
}

class Bird : Animal
```

```csharp
{
    public double wingSpan;

    // Constructor for the Bird class
    public Bird(string birdName, int birdAge,
double birdWingSpan) : base(birdName, birdAge)
    {
        wingSpan = birdWingSpan;
    }

    public override void Speak()
    {
        Console.WriteLine("The bird chirps.");
    }
}
```

In this example:

- **Animal** is the base class, and it defines common properties (name and age) and a virtual Speak() method.
- **Dog**, **Cat**, and **Bird** are derived classes that inherit from **Animal** and provide specific implementations of the Speak() method.

Creating Objects of Different Animal Classes

csharp

```csharp
class Program
```

```
{
    static void Main()
    {
        // Creating objects for different animals
        Dog    dog    =    new    Dog("Buddy",    4,
"Labrador");
        Cat    cat    =    new    Cat("Whiskers",    2,
"Black");
        Bird bird = new Bird("Tweety", 1, 0.5);

        // Displaying details and calling the
Speak method for each animal
        dog.Speak();
        cat.Speak();
        bird.Speak();
    }
}
```

The output will be:

bash

```
The Labrador dog barks.
The cat meows.
The bird chirps.
```

This demonstrates how different types of animals, all derived from the Animal base class, can have their own implementations of the Speak() method.

*Summary*

In this chapter, we explored **inheritance** in C#, which allows you to create **derived classes** that reuse and extend the functionality of a **base class**. The key points we covered are:

- **Basic inheritance** enables code reuse and extensibility.
- **Base and derived classes** are created using the : `baseClassName` syntax.
- We used a real-world **Animal class hierarchy** to demonstrate how inheritance works in C#.
- **Method overriding** allows derived classes to provide specific implementations for inherited methods.

Inheritance helps organize and manage code more efficiently, making it easier to extend and maintain in larger applications.

# CHAPTER 8

# *POLYMORPHISM: ONE INTERFACE, MANY IMPLEMENTATIONS*

Polymorphism is one of the cornerstones of Object-Oriented Programming (OOP). It allows objects of different types to be treated as objects of a common base type, enabling flexibility and extensibility in your code. In this chapter, we'll dive into the two main types of polymorphism in C#—**method overriding** and **method overloading**—and also explore **abstract classes** and **interfaces**. Finally, we'll apply these concepts in a real-world example using **Shape classes** like `Circle`, `Rectangle`, etc.

---

*What is Polymorphism?*

Polymorphism allows methods to behave differently based on the object calling them. The term **polymorphism** means "many shapes." It enables you to write code that works with objects of different types through a common interface, yet the behavior can vary based on the actual object type.

There are two main types of polymorphism in C#:

1. **Compile-time polymorphism** (also known as **method overloading**).

2. **Run-time polymorphism** (also known as **method overriding**).

Let's take a deeper look at both.

---

*Method Overriding vs. Method Overloading*

While both **method overriding** and **method overloading** are forms of polymorphism, they differ in how they're used and when they occur.

---

Method Overloading (Compile-Time Polymorphism)

**Method overloading** allows multiple methods with the same name but different parameter lists to exist in the same class. The compiler determines which method to call based on the number or type of arguments passed to the method.

- **When to use**: When you want to perform the same operation with different types or numbers of arguments.

**Example of Method Overloading:**

csharp

```csharp
class Calculator
{
    // Overloaded Add method with two integer
parameters
    public int Add(int a, int b)
    {
        return a + b;
    }

    // Overloaded Add method with three integer
parameters
    public int Add(int a, int b, int c)
    {
        return a + b + c;
    }

    // Overloaded Add method with two double
parameters
    public double Add(double a, double b)
    {
        return a + b;
    }
}

class Program
{
    static void Main()
    {
```

```
        Calculator    calculator    =    new
Calculator();

        // Calling different overloaded methods
        Console.WriteLine(calculator.Add(5,
10));        // Calls the two-parameter method
        Console.WriteLine(calculator.Add(5,   10,
15));    // Calls the three-parameter method
        Console.WriteLine(calculator.Add(5.5,
10.5));        // Calls the two-parameter double
method
    }
}
```

Output:


```
15
30
16
```

In this example, the Add method is overloaded to accept different numbers and types of parameters.

Method Overriding (Run-Time Polymorphism)

**Method overriding** allows a derived class to provide its own implementation of a method that is already defined in the base class. This type of polymorphism occurs at **runtime**, meaning the decision of which method to call is made when the program is running based on the object's actual type.

- **When to use**: When you want derived classes to implement their specific behavior while still using a common method signature defined in the base class.

**Example of Method Overriding:**

csharp

```
class Animal
{
    public virtual void Speak()    // Virtual
method allows overriding
    {
        Console.WriteLine("The   animal   makes   a
sound.");
    }
}


class Dog : Animal
{
    public override void Speak()    // Overriding
the base class method
    {
        Console.WriteLine("The dog barks.");
    }
```

```csharp
}

class Cat : Animal
{
    public override void Speak()   // Overriding
the base class method
    {
        Console.WriteLine("The cat meows.");
    }
}

class Program
{
    static void Main()
    {
        Animal myAnimal = new Animal();
        Animal myDog = new Dog();  // Dog object
assigned to Animal reference
        Animal myCat = new Cat();  // Cat object
assigned to Animal reference

        myAnimal.Speak();    // Calls  Animal's
Speak method
        myDog.Speak();       // Calls Dog's Speak
method
        myCat.Speak();       // Calls Cat's Speak
method
    }
}
```

Output:

```
bash
```

```
The animal makes a sound.
The dog barks.
The cat meows.
```

In this case, the method `Speak()` is overridden by the `Dog` and `Cat` classes, providing their own implementation of the method. The base class `Animal` defines the general behavior, and the derived classes define their specific behaviors.

---

*Abstract Classes and Interfaces*

Both **abstract classes** and **interfaces** allow you to define contracts for other classes to implement, but they serve different purposes and have different behaviors.

---

Abstract Classes

An **abstract class** is a class that cannot be instantiated on its own. It provides a base class for other classes to inherit from. Abstract classes can contain abstract methods (without implementation) as well as regular methods (with implementation).

- **Use case**: When you want to define a common interface and shared functionality, but also allow derived classes to provide specific implementations for certain methods.

**Example of an Abstract Class:**

```csharp
abstract class Shape
{
    public abstract double Area();  // Abstract method with no implementation

    public void DisplayShapeInfo()
    {
        Console.WriteLine("This is a shape.");
    }
}

class Circle : Shape
{
    public double radius;

    public Circle(double r)
    {
        radius = r;
    }
```

```csharp
    public override double Area()  // Overriding
abstract method
    {
        return Math.PI * radius * radius;
    }
}


class Rectangle : Shape
{
    public double width;
    public double height;

    public Rectangle(double w, double h)
    {
        width = w;
        height = h;
    }

    public override double Area()  // Overriding
abstract method
    {
        return width * height;
    }
}
```

In this example, the Shape class is abstract and defines an abstract
method Area(). The Circle and Rectangle classes inherit
from Shape and provide their own implementations of Area().

## Interfaces

An **interface** defines a contract that classes must follow, specifying what methods and properties the implementing classes must have. Interfaces can't have any implementation—just method signatures.

- **Use case**: When you want to define a contract that any class can implement, but you don't want to enforce any shared functionality.

**Example of an Interface:**

csharp

```csharp
interface IDrawable
{
    void Draw();   // Interface method without implementation
}

class Circle : IDrawable
{
    public double radius;

    public Circle(double r)
    {
        radius = r;
```

```csharp
    }

    public void Draw()   // Implementing Draw
method from IDrawable interface
    {
        Console.WriteLine("Drawing a circle with
radius " + radius);
    }
}

class Rectangle : IDrawable
{
    public double width;
    public double height;

    public Rectangle(double w, double h)
    {
        width = w;
        height = h;
    }

    public void Draw()   // Implementing Draw
method from IDrawable interface
    {
        Console.WriteLine("Drawing a   rectangle
with width " + width + " and height " + height);
    }
}
```

Here, `IDrawable` is an interface that defines a contract for drawing shapes. Both `Circle` and `Rectangle` implement the `Draw()` method defined in the `IDrawable` interface.

*Real-World Example: Shape Classes (Circle, Rectangle, etc.)*

Now, let's apply what we've learned about polymorphism, abstract classes, and interfaces to a real-world example involving shape classes.

```csharp
class Program
{
    static void Main()
    {
        Shape circle = new Circle(5);  // Circle
object
        Shape rectangle = new Rectangle(10, 20);
// Rectangle object

        // Displaying area for different shapes
        Console.WriteLine("Circle    area:   "   +
circle.Area());
        Console.WriteLine("Rectangle   area:   "   +
rectangle.Area());
```

```
        // Using Draw method from the IDrawable
interface
        IDrawable    drawableCircle    =    new
Circle(5);
        IDrawable    drawableRectangle    =    new
Rectangle(10, 20);
        drawableCircle.Draw();
        drawableRectangle.Draw();
    }
}
```

Output:

pgsql

```
Circle area: 78.53981633974483
Rectangle area: 200
Drawing a circle with radius 5
Drawing a rectangle with width 10 and height 20
```

In this example:

- The Shape class is abstract, and Circle and Rectangle provide their own implementations of the Area() method.
- Both Circle and Rectangle implement the IDrawable interface to provide their own Draw() method.

- Polymorphism allows us to treat different shapes (`Circle` and `Rectangle`) as `Shape` objects while still calling their specific methods (`Area()` and `Draw()`).

---

*Summary*

In this chapter, we learned about **polymorphism** in C#:

- **Method overloading** allows multiple methods with the same name but different parameters in the same class.
- **Method overriding** allows derived classes to provide their own implementation of a method defined in a base class.
- **Abstract classes** allow you to define common functionality while leaving some methods for derived classes to implement.
- **Interfaces** define a contract that implementing classes must follow, without enforcing any shared functionality.

We applied these concepts in a real-world example of **Shape classes** such as `Circle` and `Rectangle`, showing how polymorphism allows us to work with different shapes in a flexible and extensible way.

# CHAPTER 9

# INTERFACES: DEFINING A CONTRACT

In this chapter, we will explore **interfaces** in C#, which play a crucial role in defining contracts that classes must adhere to. Interfaces are essential for creating flexible, extensible, and maintainable code. We'll cover what interfaces are, how to implement multiple interfaces in a class, and a real-world example of a **logging system** using interfaces.

---

*What are Interfaces?*

An **interface** in C# is a contract that defines a set of method signatures (and sometimes properties) that a class must implement. An interface does not contain any implementation—only the method declarations. It is up to the class that implements the interface to provide the actual implementation for the methods.

Key points about interfaces:

- Interfaces cannot contain any implementation—only method signatures.

- A class that implements an interface must provide an implementation for all the methods declared in the interface.
- Interfaces allow classes to be more flexible and decoupled from the concrete implementation, leading to more maintainable code.

Here's the basic syntax for defining an interface:

csharp

```csharp
public interface IShape
{
    double Area();    // Method signature (no
implementation)
    double Perimeter();    // Another method
signature
}
```

In this example, IShape is an interface that defines two methods, Area() and Perimeter(), but it doesn't provide their implementation. Any class that implements IShape will need to define how to calculate the area and perimeter.

*Implementing Interfaces*

When a class implements an interface, it must provide concrete implementations for all the methods declared by the interface. You use the : `interfaceName` syntax in the class definition to implement an interface.

Here's an example of a `Rectangle` class implementing the `IShape` interface:

```csharp
public class Rectangle : IShape
{
    public double Width { get; set; }
    public double Height { get; set; }

    // Implementing the Area method from IShape
interface
    public double Area()
    {
        return Width * Height;
    }

    // Implementing the Perimeter method from
IShape interface
    public double Perimeter()
    {
        return 2 * (Width + Height);
```

```
    }
}
```

In this example:

- The `Rectangle` class implements the `IShape` interface and provides specific implementations for the `Area()` and `Perimeter()` methods.

---

*Implementing Multiple Interfaces*

One of the powerful features of C# interfaces is that a class can implement **multiple interfaces**. This allows you to design your classes to fulfill multiple roles by adhering to multiple contracts. A class can implement any number of interfaces, and it must provide an implementation for all methods declared in those interfaces.

Here's how you can implement multiple interfaces in a single class:

csharp

```csharp
public interface IShape
{
    double Area();
    double Perimeter();
}
```

103

```csharp
public interface IDrawable
{
    void Draw();
}

public class Rectangle : IShape, IDrawable
{
    public double Width { get; set; }
    public double Height { get; set; }

    // Implementing methods from IShape interface
    public double Area()
    {
        return Width * Height;
    }

    public double Perimeter()
    {
        return 2 * (Width + Height);
    }

    //  Implementing  method  from  IDrawable
interface
    public void Draw()
    {
        Console.WriteLine("Drawing          a
rectangle.");
    }
```

}

In this example:

- The `Rectangle` class implements both the `IShape` and `IDrawable` interfaces.
- It provides implementations for all methods declared in both interfaces.

---

*Real-World Example: Logging System with Interfaces*

Now that we have a solid understanding of interfaces, let's apply them to a real-world example—a **logging system**. In many applications, logging is an essential feature, and you might want to allow different types of logging mechanisms (e.g., logging to a file, a database, or a console).

We'll define an interface for logging and then create classes for different logging strategies (e.g., file logging, console logging).

---

Defining the Logging Interface

First, let's define an interface `ILogger` that specifies the contract for any logging class:

csharp

```csharp
public interface ILogger
{
    void Log(string message);    // Method for
logging messages
}
```

The `ILogger` interface defines a `Log()` method, which takes a string message as an argument. Any class that implements this interface will need to provide its own implementation for the `Log()` method.

---

Implementing Different Logging Strategies

Now, let's implement a few different classes that log messages in different ways. We will have `FileLogger` (logs to a file) and `ConsoleLogger` (logs to the console).

csharp

```csharp
public class FileLogger : ILogger
{
    public void Log(string message)
    {
        // Simulating logging to a file (in
reality, you would write to a file)
        Console.WriteLine($"Logging    to    file:
{message}");
```

```
    }
}

public class ConsoleLogger : ILogger
{
    public void Log(string message)
    {
        // Logging to the console
        Console.WriteLine($"Logging to console:
{message}");
    }
}
```

In this example:

- **FileLogger** logs messages as if writing to a file (you can replace the `Console.WriteLine()` with actual file-writing logic).
- **ConsoleLogger** simply logs messages to the console.

Using Multiple Loggers in a Program

Now that we have multiple loggers that implement the `ILogger` interface, we can use them interchangeably in our application. Let's see how this works in a `Program` class.

csharp

107

```
class Program
{
    static void Main()
    {
        // Using different logging strategies
        ILogger logger = new FileLogger();
        logger.Log("This is a message logged to
a file.");

        logger = new ConsoleLogger();
        logger.Log("This is a message logged to
the console.");
    }
}
```

Output:

pgsql

```
Logging to file: This is a message logged to a
file.
Logging to console: This is a message logged to
the console.
```

In this example:

- The `logger` variable is of type `ILogger`, but it can hold references to any class that implements the `ILogger` interface (in this case, `FileLogger` and `ConsoleLogger`).

- This allows us to easily switch between different logging mechanisms without changing the rest of the code. The logging system is flexible and extensible.

*Benefits of Using Interfaces*

In the logging system example, we can see the following benefits of using interfaces:

1. **Flexibility**: The `ILogger` interface allows us to define different logging mechanisms (e.g., file logging, console logging) while using the same interface. This makes the logging system extensible—if we later need to add a `DatabaseLogger`, we can easily do so by implementing the `ILogger` interface.

2. **Decoupling**: The code that uses logging (like the `Program` class) doesn't need to know about the specifics of the logging implementation. It only needs to know about the `ILogger` interface.

3. **Testability**: Interfaces make it easy to mock or replace components for unit testing. For instance, you can mock the `ILogger` interface in tests to simulate logging behavior without actually writing to a file or console.

*Summary*

In this chapter, we explored **interfaces** in C#, which define contracts that classes must follow. Key points:

- **Interfaces** define method signatures that must be implemented by classes that use them.
- A class can implement multiple interfaces, allowing it to fulfill multiple roles.
- We created a **logging system** with different logging strategies (`FileLogger`, `ConsoleLogger`) to demonstrate the use of interfaces.

Using interfaces in your code allows for greater flexibility, extensibility, and decoupling between components. Interfaces are a crucial tool for designing clean, maintainable, and testable code.

# CHAPTER 10

# ABSTRACTION: HIDING COMPLEXITY

In this chapter, we'll explore **abstraction**, a powerful concept in Object-Oriented Programming (OOP). Abstraction allows you to hide the complexity of an object and expose only the essential features. This makes your code easier to understand and use, while providing flexibility to the underlying implementation. We will discuss **abstract classes** and **abstract methods**, explore the difference between abstract classes and interfaces, and look at a real-world example using an abstract "Vehicle" class.

---

*What is Abstraction?*

**Abstraction** is the concept of hiding the internal workings of an object and exposing only the necessary details. This helps to reduce complexity and makes it easier for developers to interact with objects without needing to understand how they work internally.

Abstraction in C# is typically implemented using **abstract classes** and **abstract methods**. These allow you to define the structure and essential functionality of a class, but leave the details to be implemented by derived classes.

An **abstract class** in C# is a class that cannot be instantiated directly. Instead, it serves as a blueprint for other classes. An **abstract method** is a method that is declared in an abstract class but does not have any implementation. The derived classes that inherit from the abstract class must provide an implementation for these abstract methods.

**Key Characteristics of Abstract Classes:**

1. **Cannot be instantiated**: You cannot create an instance of an abstract class directly. It's meant to be inherited by other classes.
2. **Abstract methods**: An abstract class can contain abstract methods, which have no body and must be implemented by derived classes.
3. **Concrete methods**: An abstract class can also contain regular (non-abstract) methods with full implementations.
4. **Inheritance**: A derived class inherits from the abstract class and provides specific implementations for the abstract methods.

Here's a simple example:

112

```csharp

abstract class Animal
{
    public string Name { get; set; }

    // Abstract method: no implementation
    public abstract void Speak();

    // Regular method: has implementation
    public void Eat()
    {
        Console.WriteLine("Eating...");
    }
}
```

In this example:

- **Speak()** is an abstract method, which has no implementation in the Animal class.
- **Eat()** is a regular method with a full implementation.
- The Animal class cannot be instantiated directly, but derived classes like Dog or Cat can inherit from Animal.

---

*Implementing Abstract Methods in Derived Classes*

A derived class that inherits from an abstract class must implement all abstract methods. If a derived class does not

113

implement all the abstract methods, the class must also be marked as abstract.

Example of a derived class:

csharp

```csharp
class Dog : Animal
{
    public override void Speak()  // Implementing
the abstract method
    {
        Console.WriteLine("The dog barks.");
    }
}

class Cat : Animal
{
    public override void Speak()  // Implementing
the abstract method
    {
        Console.WriteLine("The cat meows.");
    }
}
```

In this example:

- The Dog class provides its own implementation of the Speak() method, as required by the Animal class.

- The `Cat` class also provides its own implementation of `Speak()`.

Now, we can use these classes in a `Program` class:

csharp

```
class Program
{
    static void Main()
    {
        Animal dog = new Dog();
        dog.Name = "Buddy";
        Console.WriteLine($"{dog.Name}:");
        dog.Speak();   // Calls the Dog's Speak
method
        dog.Eat();     // Calls the inherited Eat
method

        Animal cat = new Cat();
        cat.Name = "Whiskers";
        Console.WriteLine($"{cat.Name}:");
        cat.Speak();   // Calls the Cat's Speak
method
        cat.Eat();     // Calls the inherited Eat
method
    }
}
```

115

Output:

```
makefile

Buddy:
The dog barks.
Eating...
Whiskers:
The cat meows.
Eating...
```

In this program:

- Both the Dog and Cat classes inherit from Animal and provide their own implementations of Speak(), but they share the Eat() method from the Animal class.

---

*Difference Between Abstract Classes and Interfaces*

While both **abstract classes** and **interfaces** are used to define a contract for derived classes, they have key differences:

| Feature | Abstract Class | Interface |
|---|---|---|
| Implementation | Can have both abstract methods (no implementation) and | Only method signatures; no implementation. |

| Feature | Abstract Class | Interface |
|---|---|---|
| | concrete methods (with implementation). | |
| Multiple Inheritance | A class can inherit from only one abstract class. | A class can implement multiple interfaces. |
| Fields | Can contain fields, properties, and constructors. | Cannot contain fields or constructors. |
| Access Modifiers | Can have access modifiers like `public`, `protected`, `private` for methods and properties. | All members are implicitly `public`, and access modifiers are not allowed. |
| Use Case | Use when you want to share code among related classes. | Use when you want to define a contract for classes that may not share a common ancestor. |

*Real-World Example: Abstract "Vehicle" Class*

Let's use an **abstract class** to model a `Vehicle` system. We will define a base `Vehicle` class that includes abstract methods for different types of vehicles, and then create derived classes like `Car` and `Truck` to implement specific behaviors.

Step 1: Define the Abstract Vehicle Class
csharp

```csharp
abstract class Vehicle
{
    public string Make { get; set; }
    public string Model { get; set; }

    // Abstract method: derived classes must implement it
    public abstract void Start();

    // Concrete method: common functionality for all vehicles
    public void Stop()
    {
        Console.WriteLine("The vehicle has stopped.");
    }

    // Abstract method: derived classes must implement it
```

```
    public abstract void Drive();
}
```

In this `Vehicle` class:

- The `Start()` and `Drive()` methods are **abstract**—each derived class must implement these methods.
- The `Stop()` method is **concrete** and can be inherited directly by the derived classes.

Step 2: Implement Derived Classes

Now, we'll create a `Car` class and a `Truck` class that inherit from `Vehicle` and implement the abstract methods.

csharp

```
class Car : Vehicle
{
    public override void Start()
    {
        Console.WriteLine("The car starts with a
key.");
    }

    public override void Drive()
    {
        Console.WriteLine("The car drives on the
road.");
```

```
    }
}

class Truck : Vehicle
{
    public override void Start()
    {
        Console.WriteLine("The truck starts with
a button press.");
    }

    public override void Drive()
    {
        Console.WriteLine("The truck drives on a
highway.");
    }
}
```

Step 3: Using the Abstract and Derived Classes

In the Program class, we can create objects of Car and Truck
and use their methods.

csharp

```
class Program
{
    static void Main()
    {
```

```
        Vehicle car = new Car { Make = "Toyota",
Model = "Corolla" };
        Console.WriteLine($"{car.Make}
{car.Model}:");
        car.Start();
        car.Drive();
        car.Stop();

        Vehicle  truck  =  new  Truck  {  Make  =
"Ford", Model = "F-150" };
        Console.WriteLine($"{truck.Make}
{truck.Model}:");
        truck.Start();
        truck.Drive();
        truck.Stop();
    }
}
```

Output:

```
vbnet


Toyota Corolla:
The car starts with a key.
The car drives on the road.
The vehicle has stopped.
Ford F-150:
The truck starts with a button press.
The truck drives on a highway.
The vehicle has stopped.
```

In this example:

- The `Car` and `Truck` classes both inherit from the abstract `Vehicle` class and implement the `Start()` and `Drive()` methods in their own way.
- The `Stop()` method is inherited directly from the `Vehicle` class, as it's a common behavior for all vehicles.

---

*Summary*

In this chapter, we covered **abstraction** and how it allows us to hide the complexity of an object while exposing only the necessary details:

- **Abstract classes** provide a base for other classes to inherit from, and they can contain both abstract methods (which must be implemented by derived classes) and concrete methods (which are inherited as-is).
- **Abstract methods** are declared in abstract classes and have no implementation in the base class; derived classes must provide their own implementation.
- We also compared **abstract classes** and **interfaces**, highlighting their differences and appropriate use cases.
- We demonstrated abstraction with a real-world example of a **Vehicle** class hierarchy, where `Car` and `Truck`

implement their specific behaviors while sharing common functionality.

Abstraction helps to simplify code, promotes code reuse, and provides a clear contract for developers to follow when extending a class. Let me know if you have any questions or if you're ready to move on to the next chapter!

# CHAPTER 11

# COLLECTIONS AND DATA STRUCTURES

In this chapter, we will explore the fundamental data structures that allow you to store and manipulate collections of data in C#. We'll cover **arrays**, **lists**, and **dictionaries**, as well as introduce you to the **collections framework** in C#. Finally, we'll implement a **real-world example** of managing a list of products using these data structures.

---

## *Arrays: Storing Fixed-Size Collections*

An **array** is a simple data structure that allows you to store a collection of elements of the same type. Arrays in C# have a fixed size, meaning once an array is created, its size cannot be changed.

### Declaring and Initializing Arrays

You can declare an array in C# by specifying the type of elements followed by square brackets ( [ ] ). You can then initialize the array with values or leave it empty to fill later.

csharp

```
// Declare an array of integers
int[] numbers = new int[5];  // Array of size 5

// Initialize an array with values
string[] fruits = new string[] { "Apple",
"Banana", "Cherry" };

// Alternatively, you can omit the new keyword
and type when initializing
int[] ages = { 25, 30, 35, 40 };
```

Accessing Array Elements

You can access array elements using an index, starting at 0 for the first element:

csharp

```
Console.WriteLine(fruits[0]);      //    Outputs
"Apple"
Console.WriteLine(ages[2]);    // Outputs "35"
```

Iterating Through Arrays

To loop through an array, you can use a for loop or a foreach loop:

csharp

```
foreach (var fruit in fruits)
```

```
{
    Console.WriteLine(fruit);    // Outputs each
fruit in the array
}
```

While arrays are useful for storing a fixed number of elements, they are often limited by their static size. For more dynamic needs, **lists** and **dictionaries** provide better alternatives.

*Lists: Storing Dynamic Collections*

A **list** is a more flexible data structure that allows you to store elements in a dynamic collection. Unlike arrays, lists can grow or shrink in size as elements are added or removed.

Declaring and Initializing Lists

To use lists in C#, you need to include the System.Collections.Generic namespace, as the List<T> class is part of it. Here's how to declare and initialize a list:

```
csharp

using System.Collections.Generic;

// Create a list of strings
List<string> names = new List<string>();
```

```
// Add elements to the list
names.Add("John");
names.Add("Jane");
names.Add("Paul");
```

Accessing and Modifying List Elements

You can access and modify elements in a list using an index:

csharp

```
Console.WriteLine(names[0]);  // Outputs "John"

// Modify an element
names[1] = "Anna";
Console.WriteLine(names[1]);  // Outputs "Anna"
```

Iterating Through Lists

You can loop through a list using a `foreach` loop or a `for` loop:

csharp

```
foreach (var name in names)
{
    Console.WriteLine(name);   // Outputs each
name in the list
}
```

Common List Methods

- `Add()`: Adds an element to the list.

127

- `Remove()`: Removes the first occurrence of a specific element.
- `Contains()`: Checks if the list contains a specific element.
- `Count`: Gets the number of elements in the list.

---

*Dictionaries: Storing Key-Value Pairs*

A **dictionary** is a collection that stores elements as **key-value pairs**. Each key in the dictionary must be unique, and you can access values quickly using their keys.

Declaring and Initializing Dictionaries

Dictionaries in C# are part of the `System.Collections.Generic` namespace, and you declare them using the `Dictionary<TKey, TValue>` class:

csharp

```
using System.Collections.Generic;

// Create a dictionary with string keys and int
values
Dictionary<string, int> productPrices = new
Dictionary<string, int>();
```

```
// Add elements to the dictionary
productPrices.Add("Apple", 1);
productPrices.Add("Banana", 2);
productPrices.Add("Orange", 3);
```

Accessing Values in a Dictionary

You can access values by using their keys:

csharp

```
Console.WriteLine(productPrices["Apple"]);    //
Outputs "1"
```

Checking for Key Existence

Before accessing a value, you can check if a key exists using the `ContainsKey()` method:

csharp

```
if (productPrices.ContainsKey("Banana"))
{
    Console.WriteLine("Banana    price:    "    +
productPrices["Banana"]);
}
```

Iterating Through Dictionaries

To loop through the key-value pairs, you can use a `foreach` loop:

csharp

```
foreach (var item in productPrices)
{
    Console.WriteLine($"{item.Key}:
{item.Value}");
}
```

*Introduction to the Collections Framework*

The **collections framework** in C# is a set of classes and interfaces that provide a variety of data structures for storing and manipulating data. Collections in C# are part of the `System.Collections` and `System.Collections.Generic` namespaces.

Some common collection types include:

- **Arrays**: Fixed-size collections of elements.
- **Lists**: Dynamic arrays that can grow or shrink in size.
- **Dictionaries**: Collections of key-value pairs, where each key is unique.
- **Queues**: First-in, first-out (FIFO) collections.
- **Stacks**: Last-in, first-out (LIFO) collections.

The **generic** collections (like `List<T>`, `Dictionary<TKey, TValue>`, etc.) are more commonly used because they are type-safe, meaning you can define the data type of the elements they store (e.g., `List<int>`, `Dictionary<string, int>`).

---

*Real-World Example: Storing and Managing a List of Products*

Let's build a small program to manage a list of products. We'll use a `List<Product>` to store product details and a `Dictionary<string, Product>` to look up products by their names.

Step 1: Define the Product Class
csharp

```csharp
class Product
{
    public string Name { get; set; }
    public int Price { get; set; }
    public string Category { get; set; }

    public Product(string name, int price, string category)
    {
        Name = name;
        Price = price;
        Category = category;
    }
}
```

Step 2: Using a List to Store Products

**We'll use a `List<Product>` to store multiple products:**

csharp

```
class Program
{
    static void Main()
    {
        // Creating a list of products
        List<Product>    products    =    new
List<Product>();

        // Adding products to the list
        products.Add(new    Product("Apple",    1,
"Fruits"));
        products.Add(new    Product("Banana",    2,
"Fruits"));
        products.Add(new    Product("Shampoo",    5,
"Personal Care"));
        products.Add(new    Product("T-shirt",    15,
"Clothing"));

        // Displaying all products
        foreach (var product in products)
        {
            Console.WriteLine($"Product:
{product.Name},       Price:       {product.Price},
Category: {product.Category}");
```

```
        }
    }
}
```

Step 3: Using a Dictionary for Quick Lookup

You can also use a `Dictionary<string, Product>` to quickly look up a product by its name:

csharp

```
class Program
{
    static void Main()
    {
        // Creating a dictionary to store
products by name
        Dictionary<string,           Product>
productDictionary   =   new   Dictionary<string,
Product>();

        // Adding products to the dictionary
        productDictionary.Add("Apple",      new
Product("Apple", 1, "Fruits"));
        productDictionary.Add("Banana",     new
Product("Banana", 2, "Fruits"));
        productDictionary.Add("Shampoo",    new
Product("Shampoo", 5, "Personal Care"));
        productDictionary.Add("T-shirt",    new
Product("T-shirt", 15, "Clothing"));
```

```
// Looking up a product by name
string productName = "Apple";
if
(productDictionary.ContainsKey(productName))
        {
        var          product          =
productDictionary[productName];
        Console.WriteLine($"Found
{product.Name},     Price:     {product.Price},
Category: {product.Category}");
        }
        else
        {
        Console.WriteLine("Product          not
found.");
        }
    }
}
```

Output:

yaml

Found Apple, Price: 1, Category: Fruits

In this example:

- We store products in a List<Product> to manage a collection of products and iterate through them.

- We use a `Dictionary<string, Product>` to store products by their name and look them up quickly.

*Summary*

In this chapter, we explored different **collections** in C#:

- **Arrays**: Fixed-size collections of elements.
- **Lists**: Dynamic collections that can grow and shrink.
- **Dictionaries**: Collections of key-value pairs, ideal for quick lookups.

We also introduced you to the **collections framework** in C#, which provides a variety of data structures for different use cases. Finally, we applied these concepts in a **real-world example** to manage a list of products, showing how to store and look up product information using lists and dictionaries.

# CHAPTER 12

# ERROR HANDLING AND EXCEPTIONS

Error handling is a critical aspect of any software application. In C#, errors and unexpected situations are handled using **exceptions**, which provide a way to manage runtime errors. This chapter will introduce you to the fundamental concepts of **exception handling** using the `try`, `catch`, and `throw` keywords. We will also explore how to create **custom exceptions** to better handle specific errors. Finally, we'll work through a **real-world example** of handling file reading errors.

---

## What Are Exceptions?

An **exception** is an error that occurs during the execution of a program. When an error occurs, the program's normal flow is interrupted, and the runtime system looks for an exception handler to catch and handle the exception. If no handler is found, the program crashes.

In C#, exceptions are objects that inherit from the base `System.Exception` class. They can be thrown manually, or the runtime can throw them when an error occurs.

136

*Try, Catch, Throw Keywords*

C# uses three main keywords to handle exceptions:

1. **try**: This block is used to wrap the code that may cause an exception. It is followed by one or more catch blocks.
2. **catch**: This block catches and handles exceptions thrown in the try block. You can specify different exception types to catch specific errors.
3. **throw**: This keyword is used to throw an exception explicitly from the code.

Basic Try-Catch Block

Here's how to use the try, catch, and throw keywords:

```csharp
try
{
    int number = int.Parse("invalid");  // This will cause an exception
}
catch (FormatException ex)
{
    Console.WriteLine("Error:   Invalid   number format.");
```

```
    Console.WriteLine(ex.Message);   // Detailed
error message
}
```

In this example:

- The `try` block attempts to parse an invalid string as an integer, which causes a `FormatException`.
- The `catch` block catches the `FormatException` and handles it by printing an error message.

## Multiple Catch Blocks

You can have multiple `catch` blocks to handle different types of exceptions:

csharp

```
try
{
    int[] numbers = new int[2];
    numbers[5] = 10;   // This will cause an
IndexOutOfRangeException
}
catch (IndexOutOfRangeException ex)
{
    Console.WriteLine("Error:   Index   out   of
range.");
    Console.WriteLine(ex.Message);
```

```
}
catch (Exception ex)    // General exception
handler
{
    Console.WriteLine("An error occurred.");
    Console.WriteLine(ex.Message);
}
```

In this example:

- The first `catch` block handles an `IndexOutOfRangeException`.
- The second `catch` block is a more general handler for any other types of exceptions that may occur.

*Throwing Exceptions (Using `throw`)*

You can manually throw exceptions using the `throw` keyword. This is useful when you want to explicitly indicate that an error has occurred in your application.

csharp

```
public void CheckAge(int age)
{
    if (age < 18)
    {
```

139

```
      throw new InvalidOperationException("Age
must be at least 18.");
    }
    Console.WriteLine("Age is valid.");
}
```

In this example:

- The `CheckAge` method throws an `InvalidOperationException` if the age is less than 18.

---

*Custom Exceptions*

Sometimes, the standard exceptions provided by the .NET Framework are not sufficient for your specific use case. In such situations, you can define your own custom exception classes.

To create a custom exception, you should inherit from the `Exception` class and provide constructors that allow you to pass a custom message or other information.

Creating a Custom Exception

Here's how to define a custom exception:

csharp

```
public class AgeNotValidException : Exception
{
    public int InvalidAge { get; set; }

    public AgeNotValidException() { }

    public AgeNotValidException(string message)
: base(message) { }

    public AgeNotValidException(string message,
Exception innerException) : base(message,
innerException) { }

    public AgeNotValidException(string message,
int invalidAge) : base(message)
    {
        InvalidAge = invalidAge;
    }
}
```

In this example:

- `AgeNotValidException` is a custom exception that extends `Exception`.
- The constructor allows us to pass a message and an `invalidAge` value.

## Throwing a Custom Exception

You can throw the custom exception just like any other exception:

csharp

```csharp
public void ValidateAge(int age)
{
    if (age < 18)
    {
        throw new AgeNotValidException("Age must be 18 or older.", age);
    }
    Console.WriteLine("Age is valid.");
}
```

## Handling a Custom Exception

You can catch your custom exception just like built-in exceptions:

csharp

```csharp
try
{
    ValidateAge(15); // This will throw a custom exception
}
catch (AgeNotValidException ex)
{
    Console.WriteLine($"Error: {ex.Message}");
```

```
Console.WriteLine($"Invalid          Age:
{ex.InvalidAge}");
}
```

Output:

```
yaml
```

```
Error: Age must be 18 or older.
Invalid Age: 15
```

In this example, the custom exception `AgeNotValidException` is thrown when the age is less than 18, and we catch and handle it in the `catch` block.

---

*Real-World Example: Handling File Reading Errors*

A common scenario where error handling is important is when dealing with file I/O. Let's create an example where we read from a file, and we need to handle errors such as the file not being found or other I/O issues.

Step 1: Reading from a File with Error Handling

Here's how you can safely read from a file and handle potential errors using `try-catch` blocks:

```
csharp
```

```csharp
using System;
using System.IO;

class Program
{
    static void Main()
    {
        string filePath = "example.txt";

        try
        {
            string         fileContents        =
File.ReadAllText(filePath);
            Console.WriteLine("File content:");
            Console.WriteLine(fileContents);
        }
        catch (FileNotFoundException ex)
        {
            Console.WriteLine("Error:  File  not
found.");
            Console.WriteLine(ex.Message);
        }
        catch (UnauthorizedAccessException ex)
        {
            Console.WriteLine("Error:  Access  to
the file is denied.");
            Console.WriteLine(ex.Message);
        }
```

```
        catch (Exception ex)
        {
            Console.WriteLine("An      unexpected
error occurred.");
            Console.WriteLine(ex.Message);
        }
    }
}
```

In this example:

- We use `File.ReadAllText()` to read the contents of a file.
- The `catch` blocks handle specific exceptions such as `FileNotFoundException` and `UnauthorizedAccessException`.
- A general `catch` block handles any other unexpected errors.

Step 2: Writing to a File with Error Handling

You can also handle errors when writing to a file. Here's an example:

```
csharp

using System;
using System.IO;
```

145

```csharp
class Program
{
    static void Main()
    {
        string filePath = "output.txt";

        try
        {
            string    textToWrite    =    "Hello,
world!";
            File.WriteAllText(filePath,
textToWrite);
            Console.WriteLine("Text  written  to
file successfully.");
        }
        catch (UnauthorizedAccessException ex)
        {
            Console.WriteLine("Error: Access  to
the file is denied.");
            Console.WriteLine(ex.Message);
        }
        catch (Exception ex)
        {
            Console.WriteLine("An     unexpected
error occurred.");
            Console.WriteLine(ex.Message);
        }
    }
}
```

In this example:

- We use `File.WriteAllText()` to write text to a file.
- If there is a problem (e.g., lack of write permissions), the exception is caught and handled.

---

*Summary*

In this chapter, we learned about **error handling** and **exceptions** in C#:

- **Try-Catch Blocks**: Used to handle exceptions and maintain program flow when errors occur.
- **Throwing Exceptions**: You can throw exceptions explicitly using the `throw` keyword.
- **Custom Exceptions**: You can define your own exceptions by inheriting from the `Exception` class and adding custom properties or methods.
- **Real-World Example**: We explored handling **file reading errors**, including exceptions like `FileNotFoundException` and `UnauthorizedAccessException`, while reading and writing to files.

By using exceptions, you can ensure your application gracefully handles errors and provides meaningful feedback to users, improving its reliability and user experience.

# CHAPTER 13

# EVENTS AND DELEGATES

In this chapter, we'll dive into **delegates** and **events**, which are two powerful features in C# that enable you to implement **event-driven programming**. These features allow you to define methods that can be called in response to specific actions or events, like a user clicking a button or a process completing. We'll explore how **delegates** and **events** work in C#, and walk through a real-world example of handling a **button click event** in a graphical user interface (GUI).

*What are Delegates?*

A **delegate** is a type-safe function pointer that allows you to refer to a method in your code and call it indirectly. It defines a method signature and can hold a reference to any method that matches that signature.

In simpler terms, a delegate is a variable that holds a reference to a method. You can invoke (call) the method via the delegate, making it useful for scenarios where you want to pass methods around as parameters or event handlers.

## Declaring a Delegate

To declare a delegate in C#, you use the `delegate` keyword followed by the method signature. Here's an example:

csharp

```csharp
// Declare a delegate that takes an integer as a
parameter and returns void
public delegate void MyDelegate(int number);
```

In this case, `MyDelegate` is a delegate that can point to any method that takes an `int` as an argument and returns `void`.

## Using a Delegate

To use the delegate, you need to assign it a method that matches its signature. Then, you can invoke the method using the delegate:

csharp

```csharp
class Program
{
    // Method that matches the delegate signature
    public static void PrintNumber(int number)
    {
        Console.WriteLine("Number: " + number);
    }
```

```
static void Main()
{
    // Create an instance of the delegate and
assign the PrintNumber method to it
    MyDelegate    myDelegate    =    new
MyDelegate(PrintNumber);

    // Invoke the method via the delegate
    myDelegate(5);  // Outputs: "Number: 5"
}
}
```

In this example:

- We declare a delegate `MyDelegate` that takes an `int` as a parameter.
- We create an instance of the delegate and assign it the `PrintNumber` method.
- We invoke `PrintNumber` through the delegate.

## Multicasting Delegates

Delegates in C# can also point to multiple methods, allowing you to multicast or call multiple methods at once. You can add methods to a delegate using the += operator and invoke all of them with a single call.

csharp

151

```csharp
public delegate void MyDelegate(int number);

public static void PrintNumber(int number)
{
    Console.WriteLine("Number: " + number);
}

public static void PrintSquare(int number)
{
    Console.WriteLine("Square:  " + (number *
number));
}

static void Main()
{
    MyDelegate        myDelegate        =        new
MyDelegate(PrintNumber);
    myDelegate    +=    PrintSquare;        //    Add
PrintSquare to the delegate chain

    // Invoke both methods through the delegate
    myDelegate(5);   // Outputs: "Number: 5" and
"Square: 25"
}
```

Here:

- The `myDelegate` is multicast and calls both `PrintNumber` and `PrintSquare` when invoked.

*What are Events?*

An **event** in C# is a way to signal that something has occurred. It provides a mechanism for objects to notify other objects when certain actions or changes happen in the system. Events are typically used in scenarios where one part of your application needs to react to changes made by another part (e.g., a button click, a timer elapsing, etc.).

Events in C# are built on top of delegates. When you subscribe to an event, you're essentially telling the system to call a particular method (delegate) whenever the event is triggered.

Declaring an Event

To declare an event, you use the event keyword followed by a delegate type. For example:

csharp

```
public delegate void MyEventHandler(string message);

public class Publisher
{
    // Declare an event based on the MyEventHandler delegate
```

153

```csharp
public event MyEventHandler Notify;

// Method to trigger the event
public void TriggerEvent(string message)
{
    if (Notify != null)
    {
        Notify(message);   // Raise the event
    }
}
}
```

In this example:

- `MyEventHandler` is a delegate type that takes a `string` parameter and returns `void`.
- The `Notify` event is declared using the `event` keyword, based on the `MyEventHandler` delegate.

Subscribing to and Raising Events

Once an event is declared, other classes can **subscribe** to it, meaning they provide methods that will be called when the event is triggered. You can subscribe to an event using the += operator and unsubscribe using the -= operator.

csharp

```csharp
class Subscriber
```

```
{
    public void HandleEvent(string message)
    {
        Console.WriteLine("Event received: " +
message);
    }
}

class Program
{
    static void Main()
    {
        Publisher publisher = new Publisher();
        Subscriber    subscriber    =    new
Subscriber();

        // Subscribe to the event
        publisher.Notify                    +=
subscriber.HandleEvent;

        // Trigger the event
        publisher.TriggerEvent("Hello, Event!");

        // Output: "Event received: Hello,
Event!"
    }
}
```

In this example:

155

- The `Publisher` triggers the `Notify` event using the `TriggerEvent()` method.

- The `Subscriber` subscribes to the event and handles it with the `HandleEvent()` method.

---

*Real-World Example: Button Click Event in a GUI*

To better understand how events and delegates work together, let's look at a real-world example involving a **button click event** in a graphical user interface (GUI). In C#, this is common in Windows Forms or WPF applications, but we will use a simple console-based approach to demonstrate the concept.

Step 1: Defining the Button Class with an Event

Let's define a `Button` class that raises an event when it is clicked:

csharp

```csharp
public delegate void ClickEventHandler(object sender, EventArgs e);

public class Button
{
    public string Text { get; set; }
```

```csharp
    // Define the event based on the
ClickEventHandler delegate
    public event ClickEventHandler Click;

    // Method to simulate a button click
    public void SimulateClick()
    {
        // Raise the event when the button is
clicked
        Click?.Invoke(this, EventArgs.Empty);
    }
}
```

In this example:

- We declare a `ClickEventHandler` delegate, which defines the signature for the button's click event.
- The `Button` class has an event `Click`, which other classes can subscribe to.
- The `SimulateClick()` method raises the `Click` event when the button is clicked.

Step 2: Subscribing to the Button Click Event

Now, let's create a `Program` class that subscribes to the `Click` event and handles the button click:

csharp

157

```csharp
class Program
{
    // Event handler method
    static void OnButtonClick(object sender,
EventArgs e)
    {
        Console.WriteLine("Button clicked!");
    }

    static void Main()
    {
        // Create a Button instance
        Button button = new Button { Text =
"Click Me!" };

        // Subscribe to the Click event
        button.Click += OnButtonClick;

        // Simulate a button click
        button.SimulateClick();    // Outputs:
"Button clicked!"
    }
}
```

In this example:

- The OnButtonClick() method is the event handler that is called when the button is clicked.

- The `button.Click += OnButtonClick` line subscribes to the `Click` event.
- When the `SimulateClick()` method is called, the `OnButtonClick()` method is invoked, simulating a button click.

*Summary*

In this chapter, we covered **delegates** and **events**, which are essential for event-driven programming in C#:

- **Delegates** are type-safe function pointers that allow you to reference methods and invoke them indirectly. They are used extensively with events.
- **Events** are based on delegates and provide a way for objects to notify other objects when something has happened (e.g., a button click).
- We explored how to create custom events, subscribe to them, and trigger them from within a class.
- We also demonstrated a **real-world example** of a **button click event** using delegates and events, showing how event-driven programming works in a simple console application.

# CHAPTER 14

# LINQ (LANGUAGE INTEGRATED QUERY)

In this chapter, we will explore **LINQ** (Language Integrated Query), a powerful feature in C# that allows you to query collections in a concise and readable manner. LINQ enables querying data directly in C# using a syntax that's integrated with the language, rather than relying on SQL or other external querying languages. We will introduce LINQ, write basic queries, and work through a real-world example of querying a collection of books.

---

*Introduction to LINQ*

**LINQ** is a set of methods in C# that allow you to query, filter, and manipulate data from various data sources (like collections, databases, XML files, etc.) in a unified and readable way. With LINQ, you can write queries directly in C# code that can operate on in-memory collections such as arrays, lists, and dictionaries.

LINQ provides a way to perform operations such as:

- Filtering data (e.g., finding all books by a particular author)
- Sorting data (e.g., sorting books by publication year)
- Projecting data (e.g., extracting just the titles of books)
- Grouping data (e.g., grouping books by genre)
- Aggregating data (e.g., calculating the average price of books)

The LINQ syntax in C# can be written in two main styles:

1. **Query Syntax** (similar to SQL)
2. **Method Syntax** (using LINQ methods)

We will cover both styles and demonstrate how they can be used to query collections.

---

*Writing Basic Queries with LINQ*

Query Syntax

Query syntax is very similar to SQL, and it's a natural choice for those familiar with SQL-like queries. Here's a basic structure of a LINQ query in query syntax:

```csharp

from item in collection
where condition
```

161

```
select item
```

Let's break this down:

- `from item in collection`: Specifies the data source (a collection, array, or any other enumerable type).
- `where condition`: Filters the data based on a condition.
- `select item`: Specifies what to return from the data (it can be the whole item or just certain properties).

Example: Basic LINQ Query in Query Syntax

Suppose we have a collection of books, and we want to find all books published after 2010.

```csharp
var books = new List<Book>
{
    new Book { Title = "C# Programming", Author
= "John Smith", Year = 2015 },
    new Book { Title = "Advanced C#", Author =
"Jane Doe", Year = 2020 },
    new Book { Title = "Learn LINQ", Author =
"John Smith", Year = 2012 },
    new Book { Title = "C# for Beginners", Author
= "Emily Clark", Year = 2008 }
};
```

```csharp
var booksAfter2010 = from book in books
                     where book.Year > 2010
                     select book;

foreach (var book in booksAfter2010)
{
    Console.WriteLine($"{book.Title},
{book.Author}, {book.Year}");
}
```

Output:

```yaml
yaml


C# Programming, John Smith, 2015
Advanced C#, Jane Doe, 2020
Learn LINQ, John Smith, 2012
```

In this example:

- We use the `from` keyword to define the data source (`books`).
- The `where` clause filters the books published after 2010.
- The `select` keyword is used to return the `book` objects that meet the condition.

Method Syntax

Method syntax uses LINQ methods like `Where()`, `Select()`, `OrderBy()`, etc., and is more functionally styled. Here's the same query using method syntax:

csharp

```csharp
var booksAfter2010 = books.Where(book => book.Year > 2010);

foreach (var book in booksAfter2010)
{
    Console.WriteLine($"{book.Title}, {book.Author}, {book.Year}");
}
```

In this version:

- The `Where()` method filters the books based on the condition `book.Year > 2010`.

Other LINQ Methods

In addition to `Where()` and `Select()`, there are many other useful LINQ methods:

- `OrderBy()`: Sorts the collection.

- `GroupBy()`: Groups the collection based on a specified key.

- `First()`, `Last()`, `Single()`: Returns the first, last, or a single element based on a condition.

- `Aggregate()`: Performs a custom aggregation (e.g., sum, average).

- `Distinct()`: Removes duplicate elements from the collection.

---

*Real-World Example: Querying a Collection of Books*

Let's now build a more detailed example of querying a collection of books using LINQ. We'll create a `Book` class and perform various LINQ queries to retrieve specific data, such as books by a certain author, books published after a certain year, and books sorted by title.

Step 1: Define the Book Class

csharp

```csharp
public class Book
{
    public string Title { get; set; }
    public string Author { get; set; }
    public int Year { get; set; }
    public double Price { get; set; }
}
```

165

Step 2: Create a Collection of Books

csharp

```
List<Book> books = new List<Book>
{
    new Book { Title = "C# Programming", Author
= "John Smith", Year = 2015, Price = 29.99 },
    new Book { Title = "Advanced C#", Author =
"Jane Doe", Year = 2020, Price = 49.99 },
    new Book { Title = "Learn LINQ", Author =
"John Smith", Year = 2012, Price = 19.99 },
    new Book { Title = "C# for Beginners", Author
= "Emily Clark", Year = 2008, Price = 9.99 },
    new Book { Title = "Mastering LINQ", Author
= "John Smith", Year = 2018, Price = 39.99 },
    new Book { Title = "LINQ in Action", Author
= "Joe Brown", Year = 2017, Price = 24.99 }
};
```

Step 3: Querying Books by Author

**Let's find all books written by John Smith:**

csharp

```
var johnSmithBooks = books.Where(book =>
book.Author == "John Smith");

foreach (var book in johnSmithBooks)
{
```

```
    Console.WriteLine($"Title:      {book.Title},
Year: {book.Year}, Price: ${book.Price}");
}
```

Output:

yaml

```
Title: C# Programming, Year: 2015, Price: $29.99
Title: Learn LINQ, Year: 2012, Price: $19.99
Title: Mastering LINQ, Year: 2018, Price: $39.99
```

In this query:

- We use the `Where()` method to filter books by the author **John Smith**.

Step 4: Querying Books Published After 2010

Let's find all books published after **2010**:

csharp

```
var recentBooks = books.Where(book => book.Year
> 2010);

foreach (var book in recentBooks)
{
    Console.WriteLine($"Title:      {book.Title},
Year: {book.Year}, Author: {book.Author}");
```

}

Output:

```yaml
yaml


Title: C# Programming, Year: 2015, Author: John Smith
Title: Advanced C#, Year: 2020, Author: Jane Doe
Title: Mastering LINQ, Year: 2018, Author: John Smith
Title: LINQ in Action, Year: 2017, Author: Joe Brown
```

Step 5: Sorting Books by Title

Let's sort the books alphabetically by their titles:

```csharp
csharp


var    sortedBooks    =    books.OrderBy(book    =>
book.Title);

foreach (var book in sortedBooks)
{
    Console.WriteLine($"Title:    {book.Title},
Year: {book.Year}");
}
```

Output:

168

```yaml
yaml
```

```yaml
Title: Advanced C#, Year: 2020
Title: C# Programming, Year: 2015
Title: C# for Beginners, Year: 2008
Title: Learn LINQ, Year: 2012
Title: LINQ in Action, Year: 2017
Title: Mastering LINQ, Year: 2018
```

Step 6: Grouping Books by Author

Let's group the books by their author:

```
csharp
```

```csharp
var    groupedBooks    =    books.GroupBy(book    =>
book.Author);

foreach (var group in groupedBooks)
{
    Console.WriteLine($"Author: {group.Key}");
    foreach (var book in group)
    {
        Console.WriteLine($"              Title:
{book.Title}, Year: {book.Year}");
    }
}
```

Output:

```yaml
yaml
```

```
Author: John Smith
    Title: C# Programming, Year: 2015
    Title: Learn LINQ, Year: 2012
    Title: Mastering LINQ, Year: 2018
Author: Jane Doe
    Title: Advanced C#, Year: 2020
Author: Emily Clark
    Title: C# for Beginners, Year: 2008
Author: Joe Brown
    Title: LINQ in Action, Year: 2017
```

*Summary*

In this chapter, we introduced **LINQ** (Language Integrated Query), a powerful way to query collections in C#:

- **Query Syntax** provides an SQL-like syntax for querying data.
- **Method Syntax** uses LINQ methods like `Where()`, `OrderBy()`, and `GroupBy()` to perform operations on data.
- We explored how to query a **collection of books**, including filtering, sorting, and grouping books based on various conditions.

LINQ makes working with data in C# easy and readable, whether you're working with in-memory collections like lists and arrays, or external data sources like databases or XML files.

Let me know if you'd like to dive deeper into any LINQ concepts or move on to the next chapter!

# CHAPTER 15

# WORKING WITH FILES AND STREAMS

In this chapter, we will explore how to work with files in C# using **File input/output (I/O)** operations. Specifically, we'll focus on **StreamReader** and **StreamWriter** classes, which allow for reading from and writing to files. We will also look at a **real-world example** of writing a log file, demonstrating how to implement file handling in C#.

---

*File Input/Output (I/O)*

**File I/O** refers to the process of reading from and writing to files. In C#, file handling is primarily done using classes from the `System.IO` namespace. The `File` class provides static methods to handle simple file operations, such as creating, deleting, ing, and moving files. However, for more advanced file reading and writing operations, **streams** provide a better approach.

Streams represent an abstraction for data flow. They allow you to read or write data byte-by-byte or character-by-character.

**Two main types of file streams in C#:**

1. **File Streams**: Used for reading and writing bytes to a file.

2. **Text Streams**: Used for reading and writing characters to a file (more appropriate for working with text).

In this chapter, we will focus on **text streams**, which are particularly useful when working with human-readable files like .txt files.

---

*StreamReader and StreamWriter*

**StreamReader** and **StreamWriter** are classes in the System.IO namespace that simplify reading and writing text files in C#. They provide methods to read and write strings, lines, or entire files with ease.

StreamReader (Reading from Files)

The StreamReader class is used to read characters from a byte stream, and it automatically handles character encoding (like UTF-8 or ASCII). Here's how you can use it:

```csharp

using System;
using System.IO;

class Program
```

173

```csharp
{
    static void Main()
    {
        string filePath = "example.txt";

        try
        {
            // Create a StreamReader to read the file
            using (StreamReader reader = new StreamReader(filePath))
            {
                string line;
                while ((line = reader.ReadLine()) != null)
                {
                    Console.WriteLine(line); // Read and output each line from the file
                }
            }
        }
        catch (FileNotFoundException ex)
        {
            Console.WriteLine("Error: The file was not found.");
            Console.WriteLine(ex.Message);
        }
        catch (Exception ex)
        {
```

```
        Console.WriteLine("An       unexpected
error occurred.");
        Console.WriteLine(ex.Message);
    }
  }
}
```

In this example:

- We use StreamReader to open the file for reading.
- The ReadLine() method reads one line at a time from the file, and we continue reading until the end of the file.
- The using statement ensures that the StreamReader is properly disposed of once we're done reading.

StreamWriter (Writing to Files)

The StreamWriter class is used to write text to a file. It supports writing strings, characters, and lines of text.

```csharp
csharp

using System;
using System.IO;

class Program
{
    static void Main()
    {
```

```
    string filePath = "example.txt";

    try
    {
        // Create a StreamWriter to write to
the file
        using (StreamWriter writer = new
StreamWriter(filePath))
        {
            writer.WriteLine("Hello,
world!");  // Write a line to the file
            writer.WriteLine("This    is    a
sample file.");
            writer.WriteLine("StreamWriter
is used for writing text.");
        }

        Console.WriteLine("File      written
successfully!");
    }
    catch (Exception ex)
    {
        Console.WriteLine("An          error
occurred.");
        Console.WriteLine(ex.Message);
    }
  }
}
```

In this example:

- We use `StreamWriter` to create or open a text file for writing.
- The `WriteLine()` method writes a line of text to the file.
- The `using` statement ensures that the `StreamWriter` is disposed of properly, even if an exception occurs.

*Real-World Example: Writing a Log File*

Let's now implement a more practical example where we create a simple logging system that writes messages to a log file. This example will demonstrate how to append log messages to an existing file using `StreamWriter`.

Step 1: Define the Log File Writer

In this example, we will create a `Logger` class that writes log messages to a file. Each log entry will include a timestamp.

csharp

```
using System;
using System.IO;

public class Logger
{
    private string logFilePath;
```

177

```csharp
    public Logger(string path)
    {
        logFilePath = path;
    }

    public void Log(string message)
    {
        try
        {
            // Open the file for appending text
(create it if it doesn't exist)
            using (StreamWriter writer = new
StreamWriter(logFilePath, append: true))
            {
                // Write a log entry with a
timestamp

writer.WriteLine($"{DateTime.Now}: {message}");
            }
        }
        catch (Exception ex)
        {
            Console.WriteLine("Error writing to
log file.");
            Console.WriteLine(ex.Message);
        }
    }
}
```

In this Logger class:

- The constructor takes the log file path and initializes it.
- The Log() method appends a log message to the file, along with a timestamp. It uses StreamWriter with the append: true flag to add content without overwriting the existing file.

Step 2: Using the Logger in a Program

Now, let's use the Logger class to log some events:

csharp

```csharp
class Program
{
    static void Main()
    {
        string logFilePath = "log.txt";
        Logger logger = new Logger(logFilePath);

        // Simulate some operations and log
messages
        logger.Log("Application started.");
        logger.Log("Processing data...");
        logger.Log("Data processing completed
successfully.");
        logger.Log("Application terminated.");

        Console.WriteLine("Log file updated.");
    }
```

```
}
```

In this example:

- We create an instance of the `Logger` class, specifying the path to the log file.
- We call `logger.Log()` several times to simulate logging different events in the application.

### Step 3: Viewing the Log File

If you open the `log.txt` file after running the program, the content will look something like this:

yaml

```
2025-04-09 14:30:00: Application started.
2025-04-09 14:30:05: Processing data...
2025-04-09 14:30:10: Data processing completed
successfully.
2025-04-09 14:30:15: Application terminated.
```

The log file now contains timestamps for each log entry, and each new message is appended to the file without overwriting the previous content.

## Handling Errors During File I/O

When working with file I/O, there are several common errors that may occur:

- **FileNotFoundException**: The file does not exist.
- **UnauthorizedAccessException**: The application doesn't have permission to access the file.
- **IOException**: A generic I/O error occurred, such as disk space being full or a file being locked.

To handle these errors, we use `try-catch` blocks, as shown in the previous examples. By catching exceptions, we can gracefully handle issues like missing files, permission problems, and other unexpected errors.

## Summary

In this chapter, we learned how to work with files and streams in C#:

- **StreamReader** is used to read from files, and **StreamWriter** is used to write to files.
- We explored how to handle file reading and writing with `try-catch` blocks to manage errors.

- We created a simple **log file** using `StreamWriter`, demonstrating how to append log messages with timestamps.

File I/O is an essential skill for working with external data in many types of applications, from logging and configuration files to processing user data.

# CHAPTER 16

# GENERICS: CREATING FLEXIBLE AND REUSABLE CODE

In this chapter, we will explore **generics** in C#—a feature that allows you to create flexible, reusable, and type-safe code. Generics allow you to define classes, methods, and data structures with placeholders for types, enabling you to work with any data type while ensuring type safety at compile time. We'll walk through the basics of generics, how to create generic classes and methods, and finish with a **real-world example** of creating a **generic stack class**.

---

*What Are Generics in C#?*

Generics allow you to define classes, methods, or interfaces with **type parameters**. These type parameters are placeholders that can be replaced with specific types when the class, method, or interface is used. Generics offer two primary benefits:

1. **Type Safety**: Generics enforce type safety by ensuring that only the correct type can be used with a class or method.

2. **Code Reusability**: You can write a single class or method to work with many different types, reducing code duplication.

Without generics, you would need to write separate classes or methods for each specific type, leading to repetitive and error-prone code.

Example without Generics (Before)

Consider a `Box` class that holds an integer:

csharp

```
public class Box
{
    public int Value { get; set; }

    public Box(int value)
    {
        Value = value;
    }
}
```

If you wanted to create a `Box` that holds a string or a double, you'd have to create separate classes for each type:

csharp

```csharp
public class StringBox
{
    public string Value { get; set; }

    public StringBox(string value)
    {
        Value = value;
    }
}


public class DoubleBox
{
    public double Value { get; set; }

    public DoubleBox(double value)
    {
        Value = value;
    }
}
```

With **generics**, we can make this much more flexible.

*Creating Generic Classes and Methods*

Generic Classes

A **generic class** is a class that uses type parameters to work with any data type. Here's how you can create a generic class:

185

csharp

```
public class Box<T>
{
    public T Value { get; set; }

    public Box(T value)
    {
        Value = value;
    }
}
```

In this example:

- The class Box<T> is defined with a type parameter T. This allows the class to hold a value of any type.
- The type parameter T will be replaced with an actual type when you create an instance of the Box class.

Using a Generic Class

You can create a Box for any type by specifying the type argument:

csharp

```
Box<int> intBox = new Box<int>(5);    // Box for integers
```

186

```
Box<string> strBox = new Box<string>("Hello");
// Box for strings

Console.WriteLine(intBox.Value);  // Outputs: 5
Console.WriteLine(strBox.Value);    // Outputs:
Hello
```

In this example:

- Box<int> is a Box that holds an integer.
- Box<string> is a Box that holds a string.

Generic Methods

Similarly, you can create **generic methods** that can work with any type. Here's an example:

csharp

```
public class Printer
{
    public void Print<T>(T value)
    {
        Console.WriteLine(value);
    }
}
```

In this example:

- The `Print` method is a generic method that can print any type of value.

Using a Generic Method

csharp

```
Printer printer = new Printer();

printer.Print(123);        // Prints: 123
printer.Print("Hello");    // Prints: Hello
printer.Print(45.67);      // Prints: 45.67
```

In this example, the `Print` method can handle `int`, `string`, `double`, or any other type.

---

*Real-World Example: Generic Stack Class*

Now let's build a **generic stack class**. A stack is a data structure that follows the **Last In, First Out (LIFO)** principle. We'll use generics to create a stack that can store any type of element.

Step 1: Define the Generic Stack Class

Here's how you can define a simple generic stack class:

csharp

```
public class Stack<T>
```

```csharp
{
    private T[] elements;
    private int count;

    public Stack(int capacity)
    {
        elements = new T[capacity];
        count = 0;
    }

    public void Push(T item)
    {
        if (count == elements.Length)
        {
            throw                                    new
InvalidOperationException("Stack is full");
        }
        elements[count++] = item;
    }

    public T Pop()
    {
        if (count == 0)
        {
            throw                                    new
InvalidOperationException("Stack is empty");
        }
        return elements[--count];
    }
```

```
    public T Peek()
    {
        if (count == 0)
        {
            throw                          new
InvalidOperationException("Stack is empty");
        }
        return elements[count - 1];
    }

    public int Count => count;
}
```

In this example:

- The `Stack<T>` class uses a type parameter `T`, so it can hold any type of item.
- The `Push` method adds an item to the stack.
- The `Pop` method removes and returns the top item from the stack.
- The `Peek` method returns the top item without removing it.
- The `Count` property returns the number of items in the stack.

Step 2: Using the Generic Stack Class

Now, let's use the `Stack<T>` class with different types of data:

190

```csharp
csharp

class Program
{
    static void Main()
    {
        // Create a stack of integers
        Stack<int> intStack = new Stack<int>(5);
        intStack.Push(10);
        intStack.Push(20);
        intStack.Push(30);

        Console.WriteLine($"Top                   item: {intStack.Peek()}"); // Output: 30
        Console.WriteLine($"Items    in    stack: {intStack.Count}"); // Output: 3
        Console.WriteLine($"Popped             item: {intStack.Pop()}"); // Output: 30
        Console.WriteLine($"Items    in    stack: {intStack.Count}"); // Output: 2

        // Create a stack of strings
        Stack<string>    stringStack    =    new Stack<string>(5);
        stringStack.Push("Apple");
        stringStack.Push("Banana");
        stringStack.Push("Cherry");
```

191

```
        Console.WriteLine($"Top            item:
{stringStack.Peek()}"); // Output: Cherry
        Console.WriteLine($"Popped          item:
{stringStack.Pop()}"); // Output: Cherry
    }
}
```

In this example:

- We create two instances of the `Stack<T>` class—one for `int` and another for `string`.
- We use the `Push`, `Pop`, and `Peek` methods to interact with the stack.

Output:

yaml

```
Top item: 30
Items in stack: 3
Popped item: 30
Items in stack: 2
Top item: Cherry
Popped item: Cherry
```

Step 3: Advantages of Using a Generic Stack

- **Type Safety**: We cannot accidentally push a string onto an `int` stack or vice versa. The compiler will enforce that the correct type is used.

192

- **Reusability**: The `Stack<T>` class can be used with any type, making it highly reusable. You don't need to write a separate stack class for each data type.

---

*Summary*

In this chapter, we covered **generics** in C# and how they help create flexible, reusable, and type-safe code:

- **Generic classes** allow you to create classes that work with any data type.
- **Generic methods** allow you to write methods that can operate on any type.
- We created a **generic stack class** to demonstrate the power of generics and showed how to use it with different types of data.
- Generics provide **type safety** and **code reusability**, making your code more maintainable and less error-prone.

# CHAPTER 17

# REFLECTION: INSPECTING TYPES AT RUNTIME

In this chapter, we will explore **reflection** in C#, a powerful feature that allows you to inspect, analyze, and interact with types (classes, properties, methods, etc.) at runtime. Reflection can be useful for a variety of tasks such as dynamically loading types, invoking methods, or retrieving metadata about assemblies and types. We'll discuss the basics of reflection, its practical uses, and walk through a real-world example of inspecting object properties dynamically.

---

*What is Reflection in C#?*

**Reflection** is the ability of a program to inspect and manipulate the structure of objects, types, and assemblies during runtime. In C#, the `System.Reflection` namespace provides classes that allow you to examine metadata about assemblies, modules, types, members (properties, fields, methods), and more.

Reflection can be used to:

1.  Inspect types and their members (methods, properties, fields).

2.  Dynamically invoke methods or access properties and fields.

3.  Retrieve attributes associated with types and members.

4.  Create instances of types dynamically.

Reflection is often used in scenarios such as:

- Serialization and deserialization frameworks (e.g., converting objects to/from JSON or XML).
- Dependency injection frameworks.
- Debugging and logging frameworks.
- Testing frameworks that need to access private members.

*How Reflection Works in C#*

To use reflection in C#, you typically use the following core classes from the `System.Reflection` namespace:

- **Type**: Represents metadata about a type (class, interface, etc.).
- **MethodInfo**: Represents metadata about methods.
- **PropertyInfo**: Represents metadata about properties.
- **FieldInfo**: Represents metadata about fields.

- **Assembly**: Represents metadata about the assembly containing the types.

You can obtain a `Type` object by calling the `GetType()` method on an instance of a class or by using the `typeof()` operator for static types.

Basic Reflection Example

Let's start by using reflection to inspect a type at runtime:

csharp

```
using System;
using System.Reflection;

public class Person
{
    public string Name { get; set; }
    public int Age { get; set; }

    public void Greet()
    {
        Console.WriteLine($"Hello, my name is
{Name} and I'm {Age} years old.");
    }
}

class Program
```

```csharp
{
    static void Main()
    {
        Person person = new Person { Name = "John", Age = 30 };

        // Get the type of the object
        Type personType = person.GetType();

        // Display the name of the type
        Console.WriteLine("Type: " + personType.Name);  // Outputs: Person

        // Get and display properties of the type
        PropertyInfo[] properties = personType.GetProperties();
        foreach (var property in properties)
        {
            Console.WriteLine("Property: " + property.Name);
        }

        // Get and display methods of the type
        MethodInfo[] methods = personType.GetMethods();
        foreach (var method in methods)
        {
            Console.WriteLine("Method: " + method.Name);
```

```
        }
    }
}
```

Output:

vbnet

```
Type: Person
Property: Name
Property: Age
Method: Greet
Method: ToString
Method: GetType
Method: Equals
Method: GetHashCode
```

In this example:

- We use `GetType()` to obtain the `Type` object representing the `Person` class.
- We retrieve the properties (`Name`, `Age`) and methods (`Greet`, `ToString`, etc.) of the `Person` class using reflection.
- `PropertyInfo` and `MethodInfo` are used to represent metadata about properties and methods, respectively.

*Practical Uses of Reflection*

Reflection is a powerful tool that can be used in various scenarios. Here are some practical uses of reflection:

## 1. Invoking Methods Dynamically

You can use reflection to invoke methods dynamically at runtime, which can be useful in scenarios like dynamic proxies or scripting environments.

```csharp
using System;
using System.Reflection;

public class Calculator
{
    public int Add(int a, int b)
    {
        return a + b;
    }
}

class Program
{
    static void Main()
    {
```

```
        Calculator     calculator     =     new
Calculator();
        MethodInfo           method           =
typeof(Calculator).GetMethod("Add");


        // Invoke the method dynamically
        object              result           =
method.Invoke(calculator, new object[] { 10, 20
});
        Console.WriteLine("Result: " + result);
// Outputs: Result: 30
    }
}
```

In this example:

- We use `GetMethod()` to obtain the `MethodInfo` object for the `Add` method.
- The `Invoke()` method is used to call the `Add` method dynamically.

### 2. Accessing Properties and Fields Dynamically

Reflection allows you to read and write properties or fields even if you don't know their names at compile time. This can be useful for frameworks like ORMs (Object-Relational Mappers), serialization, or deserialization.

```
csharp
```

```csharp
using System;
using System.Reflection;

public class Person
{
    public string Name { get; set; }
    public int Age { get; set; }
}

class Program
{
    static void Main()
    {
        Person person = new Person();

        // Set property values dynamically
        PropertyInfo nameProperty =
typeof(Person).GetProperty("Name");
        nameProperty.SetValue(person, "John");

        PropertyInfo ageProperty =
typeof(Person).GetProperty("Age");
        ageProperty.SetValue(person, 30);

        Console.WriteLine($"{person.Name} is
{person.Age} years old.");  // Outputs: John is
30 years old.
    }
```

}

In this example:

- We use reflection to dynamically set the `Name` and `Age` properties of the `Person` object.

## 3. Inspecting Attributes

Attributes are metadata that can be added to types, methods, properties, etc., in C#. Reflection allows you to inspect these attributes at runtime.

csharp

```
using System;
using System.Reflection;

[AttributeUsage(AttributeTargets.Class)]
public class AuthorAttribute : Attribute
{
    public string Name { get; }

    public AuthorAttribute(string name)
    {
        Name = name;
    }
}
```

```csharp
[Author("John Doe")]
public class Book
{
    public string Title { get; set; }
}

class Program
{
    static void Main()
    {
        Type bookType = typeof(Book);
        object[] attributes = bookType.GetCustomAttributes(typeof(AuthorAttribute), false);

        if (attributes.Length > 0)
        {
            AuthorAttribute author = (AuthorAttribute)attributes[0];
            Console.WriteLine("Author: " + author.Name);  // Outputs: Author: John Doe
        }
    }
}
```

In this example:

- We define an `AuthorAttribute` and apply it to the `Book` class.

203

- Using reflection, we retrieve the `AuthorAttribute` and access its properties.

---

*Real-World Example: Inspecting Object Properties Dynamically*

Let's build a real-world example where we dynamically inspect and display the properties of a given object. This can be useful in scenarios like creating dynamic forms or displaying object data without knowing the structure in advance.

csharp

```csharp
using System;
using System.Reflection;

public class Product
{
    public string Name { get; set; }
    public double Price { get; set; }
    public int Stock { get; set; }

    public Product(string name, double price, int stock)
    {
        Name = name;
        Price = price;
        Stock = stock;
    }
```

```csharp
}

class Program
{
    static void Main()
    {
        Product product = new Product("Laptop",
999.99, 50);

        // Get the type of the object
        Type productType = product.GetType();

        // Get the properties of the type
        PropertyInfo[]        properties      =
productType.GetProperties();

        Console.WriteLine("Product Details:");
        foreach (var property in properties)
        {
            // Display the property name and its
value
            object          value           =
property.GetValue(product);

Console.WriteLine($"{property.Name}: {value}");
        }
    }
}
```

Output:

```
yaml

Product Details:
Name: Laptop
Price: 999.99
Stock: 50
```

In this example:

- We create a `Product` object and use reflection to inspect its properties (`Name`, `Price`, and `Stock`).
- We dynamically retrieve the value of each property using the `GetValue()` method and print it.

---

*Summary*

In this chapter, we explored **reflection** in C# and how it allows you to inspect and interact with types at runtime:

- **Reflection** provides the ability to inspect types, methods, properties, and fields dynamically.
- We covered the core classes from the `System.Reflection` namespace, such as `Type`, `MethodInfo`, and `PropertyInfo`.
- We demonstrated practical uses of reflection, including invoking methods dynamically, accessing properties and fields, and working with custom attributes.

- We built a real-world example of dynamically inspecting object properties, which can be useful for many dynamic scenarios like serialization or creating dynamic user interfaces.

Reflection is a powerful feature, but it should be used judiciously, as it can incur performance overhead and make code harder to maintain if overused.

# *CHAPTER 18*

# *ATTRIBUTES AND METADATA*

In this chapter, we will explore **attributes** in C#, which are a powerful mechanism for adding metadata to types, methods, properties, and other code elements. Attributes are used to annotate elements in your code with additional information, which can be inspected at runtime using **reflection**. We will also see how to create **custom attributes** and use them to solve real-world problems, such as **validating a model class**.

---

*What Are Attributes in C#?*

An **attribute** is a form of metadata that provides additional information about a program element (like a class, method, or property). Attributes are used to specify properties, behaviors, or other information about the elements they are applied to. In C#, attributes are applied to code elements using square brackets ( [ ] ).

Attributes can be:

- **System-defined**: C# provides many built-in attributes, such as `[Obsolete]`, `[Serializable]`, and `[NonSerialized]`.

- **Custom-defined**: You can define your own attributes to meet specific requirements.

## Using Built-in Attributes

For example, you can use the [Obsolete] attribute to mark methods or classes that are outdated:

csharp

```
[Obsolete("This    method    is    deprecated,    use
NewMethod instead.")]
public void OldMethod()
{
    // Old implementation
}

public void NewMethod()
{
    // New implementation
}
```

In this case:

- The [Obsolete] attribute is applied to the OldMethod method.
- The attribute informs developers that this method is deprecated, and a message suggests using NewMethod instead.

When this code is used, the compiler will display a warning when `OldMethod()` is called.

---

*Creating Custom Attributes*

You can define your own custom attributes by creating a class that inherits from the `System.Attribute` class. A custom attribute can be applied to types, methods, properties, and other program elements.

Defining a Custom Attribute

Here's an example of defining a custom attribute:

csharp

```
[AttributeUsage(AttributeTargets.Class          |
AttributeTargets.Method)]
public class AuthorAttribute : Attribute
{
    public string Name { get; }
    public string Date { get; }

    public AuthorAttribute(string name, string date)
    {
        Name = name;
        Date = date;
```

```
    }
}
```

In this example:

- We define the `AuthorAttribute` class, which inherits from `Attribute`.
- The `AuthorAttribute` class has two properties: `Name` and `Date`.
- The `AttributeUsage` attribute specifies that this custom attribute can be applied to classes and methods.

### Using a Custom Attribute

Now, let's apply the `AuthorAttribute` to a class and a method:

csharp

```csharp
[Author("John Doe", "2025-04-01")]
public class Book
{
    [Author("Jane Smith", "2025-05-01")]
    public void PrintDetails()
    {
        Console.WriteLine("Printing        book
details...");
    }
}
```

In this example:

- We apply the `AuthorAttribute` to the `Book` class and the `PrintDetails` method, passing the author's name and date as arguments.

---

*Accessing Attribute Information via Reflection*

To access the metadata provided by attributes, you can use **reflection**. This allows you to dynamically retrieve attribute data at runtime.

Here's how you can use reflection to read the `AuthorAttribute` applied to the `Book` class and `PrintDetails` method:

csharp

```csharp
using System;
using System.Reflection;

class Program
{
    static void Main()
    {
        // Get the type of the Book class
        Type bookType = typeof(Book);
```

212

```csharp
        // Get the Author attribute applied to
the class
        AuthorAttribute        classAuthor        =
(AuthorAttribute)Attribute.GetCustomAttribute(b
ookType, typeof(AuthorAttribute));
        if (classAuthor != null)
        {
            Console.WriteLine($"Class    Author:
{classAuthor.Name}, Date: {classAuthor.Date}");
        }

        // Get the method info for PrintDetails
        MethodInfo            method            =
bookType.GetMethod("PrintDetails");

        // Get the Author attribute applied to
the method
        AuthorAttribute        methodAuthor        =
(AuthorAttribute)Attribute.GetCustomAttribute(m
ethod, typeof(AuthorAttribute));
        if (methodAuthor != null)
        {
            Console.WriteLine($"Method    Author:
{methodAuthor.Name},                    Date:
{methodAuthor.Date}");
        }
    }
}
```

Output:

213

```yaml
yaml

Class Author: John Doe, Date: 2025-04-01
Method Author: Jane Smith, Date: 2025-05-01
```

In this example:

- We use `Attribute.GetCustomAttribute()` to retrieve the `AuthorAttribute` applied to the `Book` class and `PrintDetails` method.
- The attribute's data (author name and date) is then displayed.

---

*Real-World Example: Custom Validation Attributes for a Model Class*

A common real-world use of custom attributes is for **data validation**. Let's create a custom validation attribute that checks whether the value of a property meets certain criteria, such as ensuring that a string is not empty or null.

Step 1: Define the Custom Validation Attribute

First, we define a `RequiredAttribute` to validate that a string is not null or empty:

```csharp
csharp
```

```csharp
using System;

[AttributeUsage(AttributeTargets.Property,
Inherited = false, AllowMultiple = false)]
public class RequiredAttribute : Attribute
{
    public string ErrorMessage { get; }

    public          RequiredAttribute(string
errorMessage)
    {
        ErrorMessage = errorMessage;
    }
}
```

In this example:

- The `RequiredAttribute` is applied to properties (`AttributeTargets.Property`).
- It takes an error message as a parameter, which will be displayed if validation fails.

Step 2: Define a Model Class with Validation

Let's define a `Person` class with some properties, and apply the `RequiredAttribute` to ensure that certain fields are not empty.

csharp

215

```
public class Person
{
    [Required("Name is required.")]
    public string Name { get; set; }

    [Required("Email is required.")]
    public string Email { get; set; }

    public int Age { get; set; }
}
```

In this example:

- The Name and Email properties are decorated with the RequiredAttribute, ensuring that these fields are not empty.

Step 3: Implement Validation Logic

Now we write code that uses reflection to inspect the RequiredAttribute and perform validation on the model:

csharp

```
using System;
using System.Reflection;

public class Validator
```

```
{
    public static void Validate(object obj)
    {
        Type type = obj.GetType();
        PropertyInfo[]        properties      =
type.GetProperties();

        foreach (var property in properties)
        {
        // Check if the property has the
RequiredAttribute
            var            attribute         =
(RequiredAttribute)Attribute.GetCustomAttribute
(property, typeof(RequiredAttribute));

            if (attribute != null)
            {
                var            value          =
property.GetValue(obj) as string;
                if (string.IsNullOrEmpty(value))
                {

Console.WriteLine(attribute.ErrorMessage);
                }
            }
        }
    }
}
```

```
class Program
{
    static void Main()
    {
        Person person = new Person { Name = "",
Email = "test@example.com" };

        // Validate the person object
        Validator.Validate(person);
    }
}
```

Output:

```
swift
```

```
Name is required.
```

In this example:

- The `Validator.Validate()` method uses reflection to inspect the properties of the `Person` class and check for the `RequiredAttribute`.
- If a property marked with `RequiredAttribute` is null or empty, the validation message is displayed.

*Summary*

In this chapter, we explored **attributes** and how they can be used to add metadata to your code:

- **Attributes** are used to annotate types, methods, properties, and other code elements with additional information.
- **Custom attributes** can be created to solve specific problems, such as validation, logging, or metadata tagging.
- We demonstrated how to **access attribute data** using reflection.
- **Real-world example**: We built a **custom validation attribute** to validate the properties of a model class, ensuring that required fields are not empty.

Attributes are a powerful tool for enhancing your code with metadata that can be accessed dynamically at runtime, making them invaluable in frameworks like ORM (Object-Relational Mapping), validation, serialization, and more.

# CHAPTER 19

# WORKING WITH DATABASES (ADO.NET AND ENTITY FRAMEWORK)

In this chapter, we will explore two primary methods for working with databases in C#: **ADO.NET** and **Entity Framework (EF)**. These technologies allow you to interact with databases, perform CRUD operations (Create, Read, Update, Delete), and manipulate data in your application. We will discuss the basics of both approaches and finish with a real-world example of saving user data to a database.

---

*Connecting to Databases in C#*

Before you can interact with a database in C#, you need to establish a connection. Both ADO.NET and Entity Framework provide mechanisms to connect to various types of databases, such as SQL Server, MySQL, or SQLite.

1. **Connection Strings**: To connect to a database, you typically use a **connection string** that contains

information like the server name, database name, user credentials, etc.

Example connection string for SQL Server:

csharp

```
string            connectionString         =
"Server=myServerAddress;Database=myDataBase;Use
r Id=myUsername;Password=myPassword;";
```

*Introduction to ADO.NET*

**ADO.NET** (ActiveX Data Objects) is a low-level data access technology in .NET that allows you to connect to a database and execute SQL queries directly. It provides a set of classes that help you interact with databases using commands and readers.

Basic Steps to Use ADO.NET

1. **Establish a Connection**: Use `SqlConnection` (or other database-specific connection classes) to establish a connection to the database.
2. **Create a Command**: Use `SqlCommand` to execute SQL queries (SELECT, INSERT, UPDATE, DELETE).

3. **Execute the Command**: Execute the command using methods like `ExecuteReader()`, `ExecuteNonQuery()`, or `ExecuteScalar()`.

4. **Read Data**: Use `SqlDataReader` to retrieve data from the database.

5. **Close the Connection**: Always ensure to close the connection once the operations are complete.

*ADO.NET Example: Inserting User Data into a Database*

Here's an example of how to use ADO.NET to insert user data into a SQL Server database.

```csharp
using System;
using System.Data.SqlClient;

class Program
{
    static void Main()
    {
        string connectionString = "Server=myServerAddress;Database=myDataBase;User Id=myUsername;Password=myPassword;";
        string insertQuery = "INSERT INTO Users (Name, Email, Age) VALUES (@Name, @Email, @Age)";
```

```csharp
    using (SqlConnection connection = new
SqlConnection(connectionString))
    {
        SqlCommand command = new
SqlCommand(insertQuery, connection);

command.Parameters.AddWithValue("@Name",  "John
Doe");

command.Parameters.AddWithValue("@Email",
"johndoe@example.com");

command.Parameters.AddWithValue("@Age", 30);

        try
        {
            connection.Open();
            int rowsAffected =
command.ExecuteNonQuery();
            Console.WriteLine($"Rows
affected: {rowsAffected}");
        }
        catch (Exception ex)
        {
            Console.WriteLine("An    error
occurred: " + ex.Message);
        }
    }
}
```

223

```
}
```

In this example:

- We create an SQL `INSERT` query that inserts data into the `Users` table.

- We use `SqlCommand` to execute the query and `ExecuteNonQuery()` to perform the insert operation.

- The `@Name`, `@Email`, and `@Age` are parameters that protect against SQL injection.

---

*Introduction to Entity Framework (EF)*

**Entity Framework (EF)** is a higher-level ORM (Object-Relational Mapping) framework that abstracts the database interactions, allowing you to work with data as strongly-typed objects. EF maps database tables to C# classes, making database operations more intuitive and reducing the amount of boilerplate code required for interacting with databases.

Advantages of Entity Framework

- **Productivity**: EF allows you to work with objects rather than SQL queries.
- **Database Abstraction**: EF abstracts the underlying database operations, allowing you to work with database tables as C# objects.

- **Query Flexibility**: EF supports LINQ (Language Integrated Query) to query data in a more readable and type-safe manner.
- **Migrations**: EF provides built-in support for database migrations, allowing you to easily update the database schema as your model evolves.

Entity Framework Example: Saving User Data

Let's now see how to perform the same operation as in the ADO.NET example but using **Entity Framework**. We will:

1. Define a `User` model class.
2. Use **EF Core** to insert a new user into the database.

First, ensure you have the **Entity Framework Core** NuGet package installed in your project. You can install it via the NuGet Package Manager Console:

```bash
```

```
Install-Package
Microsoft.EntityFrameworkCore.SqlServer
Install-Package
Microsoft.EntityFrameworkCore.Tools
```

Step 1: Define the User Model

```csharp
```

```
using Microsoft.EntityFrameworkCore;

public class User
{
    public int Id { get; set; }
    public string Name { get; set; }
    public string Email { get; set; }
    public int Age { get; set; }
}

public class AppDbContext : DbContext
{
    public DbSet<User> Users { get; set; }

    protected            override            void
OnConfiguring(DbContextOptionsBuilder
optionsBuilder)
    {

optionsBuilder.UseSqlServer("Server=myServerAdd
ress;Database=myDataBase;User
Id=myUsername;Password=myPassword;");
    }
}
```

In this example:

- We define a User class that represents the Users table in the database.

226

- The `AppDbContext` class inherits from `DbContext`, which is the main class for interacting with the database in Entity Framework.
- The `Users` property is a `DbSet` that represents the table in the database.

Step 2: Insert a New User

Now, let's insert a new user into the database using EF Core:

csharp

```csharp
using System;

class Program
{
    static void Main()
    {
        using (var context = new AppDbContext())
        {
            var user = new User
            {
                Name = "John Doe",
                Email = "johndoe@example.com",
                Age = 30
            };

            context.Users.Add(user);
```

```
        context.SaveChanges();       // Save
changes to the database

        Console.WriteLine("User saved to the
database!");
        }
    }
}
```

In this example:

- We create a new `User` object and set its properties.
- We add the user to the `Users` table using `context.Users.Add(user)`.
- `SaveChanges()` is called to persist the changes to the database.

---

*Real-World Example: Saving User Data to a Database*

To put everything together, let's create a real-world scenario where a user fills out a form, and their data is saved to a database. This could be part of a larger application, such as a registration form for a website or a desktop application.

Step 1: Define the User Model and Context (Already Covered)
csharp

```csharp
public class User
{
    public int Id { get; set; }
    public string Name { get; set; }
    public string Email { get; set; }
    public int Age { get; set; }
}


public class AppDbContext : DbContext
{
    public DbSet<User> Users { get; set; }

    protected          override          void
OnConfiguring(DbContextOptionsBuilder
optionsBuilder)
    {

optionsBuilder.UseSqlServer("Server=myServerAdd
ress;Database=myDataBase;User
Id=myUsername;Password=myPassword;");
    }
}
```

Step 2: Create a Console Application for User Input

Now, let's create a simple console application that accepts user input and saves it to the database:

csharp

```csharp
using System;

class Program
{
    static void Main()
    {
        Console.WriteLine("Enter your name:");
        string name = Console.ReadLine();

        Console.WriteLine("Enter your email:");
        string email = Console.ReadLine();

        Console.WriteLine("Enter your age:");
        int age = int.Parse(Console.ReadLine());

        // Create a new user object
        var user = new User
        {
            Name = name,
            Email = email,
            Age = age
        };

        // Save the user to the database using
Entity Framework
        using (var context = new AppDbContext())
        {
            context.Users.Add(user);
            context.SaveChanges();
```

```
        Console.WriteLine("User    data    saved
successfully!");
        }
    }
}
```

In this example:

- The user is prompted to enter their name, email, and age.
- The input is used to create a User object.
- The User object is saved to the database using Entity Framework.

*Summary*

In this chapter, we covered **working with databases in C#** using both **ADO.NET** and **Entity Framework (EF)**:

- **ADO.NET** allows for direct SQL-based interaction with databases, providing more control over the database operations.
- **Entity Framework** is a higher-level ORM (Object-Relational Mapping) that allows you to work with databases in an object-oriented way, using classes that map to database tables.
- We demonstrated how to save user data to a database using both ADO.NET and Entity Framework.

231

Entity Framework is often the preferred choice when working with .NET applications due to its ease of use and productivity benefits, but ADO.NET is still useful when you need finer control over your database interactions.

# CHAPTER 20

# MULTITHREADING AND ASYNCHRONOUS PROGRAMMING

In this chapter, we will explore **multithreading** and **asynchronous programming** in C#. These concepts are essential for building efficient and responsive applications that can perform multiple tasks simultaneously. Multithreading allows you to run multiple threads in parallel, while asynchronous programming (using `async/await`) allows you to execute tasks without blocking the main thread. We will discuss the basics of both techniques and walk through a **real-world example** of downloading multiple files concurrently.

*Basics of Multithreading*

**Multithreading** is a technique that allows multiple threads of execution to run in parallel, making it possible to perform several tasks at the same time. Each thread can execute a separate portion of code, enabling the CPU to perform multiple operations concurrently.

233

In C#, you can create and manage threads using the `System.Threading` namespace. Here's a basic example of creating and running threads in C#:

Creating and Running Threads

csharp

```csharp
using System;
using System.Threading;

class Program
{
    static void Main()
    {
        // Create and start two threads
        Thread thread1 = new Thread(DoWork);
        Thread thread2 = new Thread(DoWork);

        thread1.Start();
        thread2.Start();
    }

    // Method to be executed on each thread
    static void DoWork()
    {
        Console.WriteLine($"Thread
{Thread.CurrentThread.ManagedThreadId}      is
working.");
    }
```

```
}
```

In this example:

- We create two `Thread` objects and pass a method (`DoWork`) to be executed on each thread.
- `Start()` is used to begin the execution of the threads.
- Each thread will execute the `DoWork` method concurrently.

## Thread Synchronization

When working with multiple threads, synchronization is essential to prevent race conditions (when multiple threads try to access shared resources simultaneously). C# provides several synchronization mechanisms, such as `lock` statements, `Mutex`, `Semaphore`, etc.

Example of using `lock` for synchronization:

csharp

```csharp
private static readonly object lockObject = new object();

static void DoWork()
{
    lock (lockObject)
    {
```

235

```
Console.WriteLine($"Thread
{Thread.CurrentThread.ManagedThreadId}          is
working.");
    }
}
```

In this example, the `lock` keyword ensures that only one thread can enter the critical section (the code inside the `lock` block) at a time.

---

*Introduction to async/await*

In C#, **asynchronous programming** allows you to run tasks without blocking the main thread. This is especially useful for I/O-bound operations like file reading, web requests, and database queries, where waiting for the result would otherwise block the execution of the application.

The **async** and **await** keywords in C# make it easier to write asynchronous code. These keywords simplify working with tasks and prevent you from dealing with callbacks or manually managing threads.

How async/await Works

- The `async` keyword is used to declare a method as asynchronous. It indicates that the method will return a `Task` (or `Task<T>`) and may contain `await` expressions.
- The `await` keyword is used inside an asynchronous method to indicate that the method should wait for a task to complete before continuing with the execution.

Here's a basic example of an asynchronous method:

csharp

```
using System;
using System.Threading.Tasks;

class Program
{
    static async Task Main()
    {
        await PerformTaskAsync();
        Console.WriteLine("Task completed.");
    }

    static async Task PerformTaskAsync()
    {
        Console.WriteLine("Task started.");
        await Task.Delay(2000);  // Simulate a 2-
second delay
```

```
        Console.WriteLine("Task finished.");
    }
}
```

In this example:

- The `PerformTaskAsync()` method is marked with `async`, indicating that it contains an asynchronous operation.
- The `await Task.Delay(2000)` simulates a non-blocking delay of 2 seconds.
- The `Main` method waits for `PerformTaskAsync()` to complete before printing "Task completed."

Advantages of async/await

- **Non-blocking**: Async methods do not block the main thread, making the application more responsive.
- **Cleaner code**: The code is easier to read and maintain compared to using callbacks or manual threading.

*Real-World Example: Downloading Multiple Files Concurrently*

Now, let's build a real-world example of downloading multiple files concurrently using **asynchronous programming**. This is useful when you need to download several files at once without

238

blocking the main thread, improving the overall performance of your application.

## Step 1: Downloading a Single File Asynchronously

We will use the HttpClient class to download files from the web asynchronously. First, let's write a method that downloads a single file asynchronously:

csharp

```csharp
using System;
using System.Net.Http;
using System.Threading.Tasks;

class Program
{
    static async Task Main()
    {
        string                  url                  =
"https://example.com/samplefile.txt";
        string filePath = "samplefile.txt";

        await DownloadFileAsync(url, filePath);
    }

    static async Task DownloadFileAsync(string
url, string filePath)
    {
```

239

```
        using    (HttpClient    client    =    new
HttpClient())
        {
            Console.WriteLine($"Downloading
{url}...");
            byte[]        fileData        =        await
client.GetByteArrayAsync(url);
            await
System.IO.File.WriteAllBytesAsync(filePath,
fileData);
            Console.WriteLine($"Download
completed: {filePath}");
        }
    }
}
```

In this example:

- We use `HttpClient.GetByteArrayAsync()` to download the file as a byte array asynchronously.
- We then save the file to the specified path using `File.WriteAllBytesAsync()`.

Step 2: Downloading Multiple Files Concurrently

Now let's modify the program to download multiple files concurrently. We'll use `Task.WhenAll()` to run multiple download tasks at the same time.

240

```csharp
csharp

using System;
using System.Net.Http;
using System.Threading.Tasks;

class Program
{
    static async Task Main()
    {
        string[] urls =
        {
            "https://example.com/file1.txt",
            "https://example.com/file2.txt",
            "https://example.com/file3.txt"
        };

        string[] fileNames = {  "file1.txt",
"file2.txt", "file3.txt" };

        // Create an array of download tasks
        Task[]       downloadTasks      =       new
Task[urls.Length];

        for (int i = 0; i < urls.Length; i++)
        {
            int index = i; // Capture the current
index for the lambda
```

241

```
            downloadTasks[i]                  =
DownloadFileAsync(urls[index],
fileNames[index]);
        }

        // Wait for all download tasks to
complete
        await Task.WhenAll(downloadTasks);
        Console.WriteLine("All files downloaded
successfully.");
    }

    static async Task DownloadFileAsync(string
url, string filePath)
    {
        using (HttpClient client = new
HttpClient())
        {
            Console.WriteLine($"Downloading
{url}...");
            byte[] fileData = await
client.GetByteArrayAsync(url);
            await
System.IO.File.WriteAllBytesAsync(filePath,
fileData);
            Console.WriteLine($"Downloaded
{filePath}");
        }
    }
```

```
}
```

In this example:

- We define an array of URLs (`urls`) and corresponding file names (`fileNames`).
- We create an array of tasks (`downloadTasks`), where each task is a download operation for a file.
- We use `Task.WhenAll()` to wait for all download tasks to complete before printing the success message.

### Advantages of Concurrent Downloads

- **Improved Performance**: By downloading multiple files concurrently, we significantly reduce the overall download time compared to downloading them sequentially.
- **Non-blocking**: Each download runs asynchronously without blocking the main thread, allowing the application to remain responsive.

---

*Summary*

In this chapter, we explored **multithreading** and **asynchronous programming** in C#:

- **Multithreading** allows you to run multiple threads concurrently, making your application more efficient, especially for CPU-bound tasks.
- **Asynchronous programming** using the `async` and `await` keywords simplifies non-blocking operations, such as I/O-bound tasks like file and network operations.
- We demonstrated a **real-world example** of downloading multiple files concurrently, showing how `async`/`await` can be used to improve performance and keep your application responsive.

Multithreading and asynchronous programming are essential tools for creating efficient applications, especially when working with I/O-bound or CPU-bound tasks that can be parallelized.

# CHAPTER 21

# DESIGN PATTERNS IN C#

In this chapter, we will explore **design patterns**—common solutions to recurring problems in software design. Design patterns provide a proven template for structuring code in a way that is efficient, flexible, and easy to maintain. In C#, design patterns are widely used to improve code reusability, scalability, and manageability. We will cover the basics of design patterns, three key design patterns—**Singleton**, **Factory**, and **Observer**—and demonstrate a real-world example using the **Singleton** pattern for managing a database connection.

## What Are Design Patterns?

A **design pattern** is a general, reusable solution to a common problem that occurs within a given context in software design. Patterns are not code implementations but templates or blueprints that can be adapted to solve specific issues in various situations.

Design patterns provide the following benefits:

- **Reusability**: Design patterns are general solutions that can be reused in different projects.

- **Efficiency**: Using a design pattern can reduce the time and effort needed to solve common design problems.
- **Maintainability**: Design patterns often improve the structure of your code, making it easier to manage and extend.
- **Communication**: Design patterns provide a shared vocabulary for developers, allowing them to communicate design decisions more clearly.

There are three primary types of design patterns:

1. **Creational Patterns**: Concerned with object creation mechanisms, trying to create objects in a manner suitable to the situation.
2. **Structural Patterns**: Concerned with the composition of classes or objects, focusing on how to compose objects to form larger structures.
3. **Behavioral Patterns**: Concerned with communication between objects and responsibility delegation.

---

*Key Design Patterns*

Here are three key design patterns we'll cover in this chapter:

1. **Singleton Pattern**
2. **Factory Pattern**
3. **Observer Pattern**

## 1. Singleton Pattern

The **Singleton** pattern ensures that a class has only one instance and provides a global access point to that instance. This pattern is useful when you want to restrict the instantiation of a class to a single object, such as when managing resources that are shared across an application (e.g., a database connection or logging system).

Implementation of the Singleton Pattern

csharp

```csharp
public class Singleton
{
    private static Singleton instance;
    private static readonly object lockObj = new object();

    // Private constructor to prevent instantiation
    private Singleton() { }

    // Public method to access the singleton instance
    public static Singleton Instance
    {
        get
        {
```

```
        // Thread-safe check to ensure only
one instance is created
        if (instance == null)
        {
            lock (lockObj)
            {
                if (instance == null)
                {
                    instance        =        new
Singleton();
                }
            }
        }
        return instance;
    }
}

    public void DoSomething()
    {
        Console.WriteLine("Singleton instance is
doing something.");
    }
}
```

In this example:

- The Singleton class has a private static variable
  instance, which holds the only instance of the class.

- The `Instance` property ensures that only one instance of the class is created and provides a global access point to that instance.
- The `lock` statement ensures that the creation of the instance is thread-safe, which is important in multithreaded applications.

Using the Singleton Pattern
csharp

```
class Program
{
    static void Main()
    {
        // Access the Singleton instance and use
its method
        Singleton            singleton            =
Singleton.Instance;
        singleton.DoSomething();
    }
}
```

Output:

csharp

Singleton instance is doing something.

249

The **Singleton** pattern ensures that only one instance of the Singleton class is created throughout the application's lifecycle, which is ideal for managing resources like a database connection.

2. Factory Pattern

The **Factory** pattern is a creational design pattern that provides an interface for creating objects, but allows subclasses or concrete implementations to decide which class to instantiate. This pattern is used to centralize object creation logic and decouple object creation from the rest of the application.

Implementation of the Factory Pattern
csharp

```csharp
public abstract class Product
{
    public abstract void Use();
}

public class ConcreteProductA : Product
{
    public override void Use()
    {
        Console.WriteLine("Using
ConcreteProductA");
    }
}
```

```csharp
public class ConcreteProductB : Product
{
    public override void Use()
    {
        Console.WriteLine("Using
ConcreteProductB");
    }
}


public abstract class Creator
{
    public abstract Product FactoryMethod();
}


public class ConcreteCreatorA : Creator
{
    public override Product FactoryMethod()
    {
        return new ConcreteProductA();
    }
}


public class ConcreteCreatorB : Creator
{
    public override Product FactoryMethod()
    {
        return new ConcreteProductB();
    }
}
```

In this example:

- The `Creator` class has a `FactoryMethod()` that defines the object creation process.
- `ConcreteCreatorA` and `ConcreteCreatorB` implement the `FactoryMethod()` to return different `Product` objects (`ConcreteProductA` or `ConcreteProductB`).

Using the Factory Pattern

csharp

```csharp
class Program
{
    static void Main()
    {
        Creator creatorA = new ConcreteCreatorA();
        Product productA = creatorA.FactoryMethod();
        productA.Use();

        Creator creatorB = new ConcreteCreatorB();
        Product productB = creatorB.FactoryMethod();
        productB.Use();
    }
}
```

Output:

```sql
Using ConcreteProductA
Using ConcreteProductB
```

The **Factory Pattern** allows you to create objects of different types without specifying the exact class to instantiate. This pattern helps centralize the object creation logic and makes it easier to manage and extend.

### 3. Observer Pattern

The **Observer** pattern is a behavioral design pattern that allows an object (called the **subject**) to notify multiple observers about changes to its state. This pattern is useful in scenarios where you need to notify many parts of your application when some event occurs, such as in event-driven systems.

### Implementation of the Observer Pattern

```csharp
using System;
using System.Collections.Generic;

public interface IObserver
{
    void Update(string message);
```

253

```csharp
}

public class ConcreteObserver : IObserver
{
    private string name;

    public ConcreteObserver(string name)
    {
        this.name = name;
    }

    public void Update(string message)
    {
        Console.WriteLine($"{name}        received
update: {message}");
    }
}

public class Subject
{
    private List<IObserver> observers = new
List<IObserver>();

    public void AddObserver(IObserver observer)
    {
        observers.Add(observer);
    }
```

```csharp
public      void      RemoveObserver(IObserver
observer)
    {
        observers.Remove(observer);
    }

    public void NotifyObservers(string message)
    {
        foreach (var observer in observers)
        {
            observer.Update(message);
        }
    }
}
```

In this example:

- The Subject class maintains a list of IObserver objects.
- The NotifyObservers() method notifies all observers when a change occurs.
- The ConcreteObserver class implements the IObserver interface to handle updates.

Using the Observer Pattern

csharp

```csharp
class Program
{
```

```
static void Main()
{
    Subject subject = new Subject();

    IObserver        observer1      =       new
ConcreteObserver("Observer 1");
    IObserver        observer2      =       new
ConcreteObserver("Observer 2");

    subject.AddObserver(observer1);
    subject.AddObserver(observer2);

    subject.NotifyObservers("State
changed!");
}
}
```

Output:

```
sql


Observer 1 received update: State changed!
Observer 2 received update: State changed!
```

The **Observer Pattern** allows multiple observers to be notified when the state of the subject changes. This pattern is useful in event-driven systems or when implementing features like UI updates in response to data changes.

*Real-World Example: Singleton Pattern for a Database Connection*

In this real-world example, we will use the **Singleton Pattern** to manage a database connection. A database connection is a shared resource, and we want to ensure that only one connection is created and reused across the application.

Step 1: Implement the Singleton Database Connection
csharp

```
public class DatabaseConnection
{
    private static DatabaseConnection instance;
    private static readonly object lockObj = new
object();

    private DatabaseConnection() { }

    public static DatabaseConnection Instance
    {
        get
        {
            if (instance == null)
            {
                lock (lockObj)
                {
                    if (instance == null)
                    {
```

257

```
                    instance       =       new
DatabaseConnection();
                }
            }
        }
        return instance;
    }
}


    public void Connect()
    {
        Console.WriteLine("Connecting    to    the
database...");
    }
}
```

Step 2: Using the Singleton Database Connection

csharp

```
class Program
{
    static void Main()
    {
        // Access the Singleton database
connection
        DatabaseConnection    dbConnection    =
DatabaseConnection.Instance;
        dbConnection.Connect();

        // Access the same instance again
```

258

```
        DatabaseConnection    sameDbConnection    =
DatabaseConnection.Instance;
        sameDbConnection.Connect();
    }
}
```

Output:

```
css


Connecting to the database...
Connecting to the database...
```

In this example:

- The `DatabaseConnection` class follows the Singleton pattern to ensure that only one instance of the database connection is created.
- We access the same instance of `DatabaseConnection` every time, ensuring efficient use of the shared resource.

---

*Summary*

In this chapter, we explored **design patterns** and how they can help create maintainable, reusable, and scalable software:

- **Singleton Pattern** ensures that a class has only one instance and provides a global access point to it.

- **Factory Pattern** provides a way to create objects without specifying the exact class to instantiate.
- **Observer Pattern** allows objects to be notified when a change occurs in another object, making it suitable for event-driven applications.

We demonstrated these patterns with real-world examples, including a **Singleton** pattern for managing a database connection.

Design patterns are essential tools for solving common problems in a standardized way, and understanding them will help you write cleaner, more maintainable code.

# CHAPTER 22

# UNIT TESTING AND TEST-DRIVEN DEVELOPMENT (TDD)

In this chapter, we will explore **unit testing** and **test-driven development (TDD)**, which are fundamental practices for ensuring the correctness and reliability of software. We will cover the basics of unit testing, demonstrate how to write unit tests in C# using **NUnit** or **MSTest**, and conclude with a **real-world example** of writing unit tests for a `Calculator` class.

---

## What is Unit Testing?

**Unit testing** is the process of testing individual units or components of a program to ensure that they behave as expected. A **unit** typically refers to a small, isolated piece of functionality, such as a method or function. The goal of unit testing is to verify that each unit of code works correctly in isolation from the rest of the application.

Key characteristics of unit tests:

- **Isolated**: A unit test tests only one piece of functionality at a time, without dependencies on other parts of the system.
- **Automated**: Unit tests are written in code and can be executed automatically, which makes it easy to test frequently during development.
- **Repeatable**: Unit tests should produce the same result every time they are run, ensuring the consistency of the functionality being tested.

Unit testing helps detect bugs early, improves the design of code, and facilitates code refactoring with confidence.

---

*Writing Unit Tests in C#*

To write unit tests in C#, you can use testing frameworks like **NUnit** or **MSTest**. These frameworks provide tools to define test cases, run them, and report the results.

1. NUnit

**NUnit** is one of the most popular testing frameworks for C#. It allows you to define test methods, arrange test data, and assert expected results.

Basic NUnit Test Example

csharp

```csharp
using NUnit.Framework;

public class Calculator
{
    public int Add(int a, int b)
    {
        return a + b;
    }

    public int Subtract(int a, int b)
    {
        return a - b;
    }
}


[TestFixture]
public class CalculatorTests
{
    private Calculator calculator;

    [SetUp]
    public void Setup()
    {
        calculator = new Calculator();
    }

    [Test]
```

```
    public                                void
Add_ReturnsCorrectSum_WhenGivenTwoNumbers()
    {
        int result = calculator.Add(2, 3);
        Assert.AreEqual(5, result);
    }


    [Test]
    public                                void
Subtract_ReturnsCorrectDifference_WhenGivenTwoN
umbers()
    {
        int result = calculator.Subtract(5, 3);
        Assert.AreEqual(2, result);
    }
}
```

In this example:

- The [TestFixture] attribute marks the CalculatorTests class as containing tests.
- The [SetUp] attribute marks the Setup() method to be executed before each test, where we initialize the Calculator object.
- The [Test] attribute marks methods as test cases, which will be executed during testing.
- The Assert.AreEqual() method checks if the actual result matches the expected result.

## Running NUnit Tests

To run NUnit tests, you can use the NUnit Console Runner or integrate NUnit with Visual Studio by installing the NUnit and NUnit3TestAdapter NuGet packages.

## 2. MSTest

**MSTest** is the default testing framework for Visual Studio and is also widely used for unit testing in C#. Like NUnit, MSTest provides similar functionality for defining and running tests.

## Basic MSTest Example

```csharp
using
Microsoft.VisualStudio.TestTools.UnitTesting;

public class Calculator
{
    public int Add(int a, int b)
    {
        return a + b;
    }

    public int Subtract(int a, int b)
    {
        return a - b;
    }
```

```csharp
}


[TestClass]
public class CalculatorTests
{
    private Calculator calculator;

    [TestInitialize]
    public void Setup()
    {
        calculator = new Calculator();
    }

    [TestMethod]
    public                                    void
Add_ReturnsCorrectSum_WhenGivenTwoNumbers()
    {
        int result = calculator.Add(2, 3);
        Assert.AreEqual(5, result);
    }

    [TestMethod]
    public                                    void
Subtract_ReturnsCorrectDifference_WhenGivenTwoN
umbers()
    {
        int result = calculator.Subtract(5, 3);
        Assert.AreEqual(2, result);
    }
```

}

In this MSTest example:

- The [TestClass] attribute marks the CalculatorTests class as containing test methods.
- The [TestInitialize] attribute marks the Setup() method to be executed before each test.
- The [TestMethod] attribute marks methods as individual test cases.
- Assert.AreEqual() is used to verify that the actual results match the expected results.

## Running MSTest Tests

MSTest is integrated into Visual Studio, so you can run tests directly within the Visual Studio Test Explorer.

## What is Test-Driven Development (TDD)?

**Test-Driven Development (TDD)** is a software development approach where you write tests before writing the actual code. The TDD cycle follows these steps:

1. **Write a test**: Write a test for a small piece of functionality you want to implement.

2. **Run the test**: Run the test and confirm that it fails (since the code isn't implemented yet).

3. **Write the code**: Implement the minimum code needed to make the test pass.

4. **Refactor**: Clean up the code and make sure the test still passes.

5. **Repeat**: Continue writing tests and implementing code in small increments.

The main goal of TDD is to ensure that your code is well-tested from the start, leading to better code quality and fewer bugs.

---

*Real-World Example: Unit Tests for a "Calculator" Class*

Let's build a simple `Calculator` class and write unit tests for its methods using **NUnit** (but the process is similar for MSTest).

Step 1: Define the Calculator Class
csharp

```csharp
public class Calculator
{
    public int Add(int a, int b)
    {
        return a + b;
    }
}
```

```csharp
    public int Subtract(int a, int b)
    {
        return a - b;
    }

    public int Multiply(int a, int b)
    {
        return a * b;
    }

    public double Divide(int a, int b)
    {
        if (b == 0) throw new
DivideByZeroException("Cannot divide by zero.");
        return (double)a / b;
    }
}
```

Step 2: Write Unit Tests for the Calculator Class

csharp

```csharp
using NUnit.Framework;

[TestFixture]
public class CalculatorTests
{
    private Calculator calculator;

    [SetUp]
    public void Setup()
```

269

```csharp
    {
        calculator = new Calculator();
    }

    [Test]
    public                              void
Add_ReturnsCorrectSum_WhenGivenTwoNumbers()
    {
        int result = calculator.Add(3, 4);
        Assert.AreEqual(7, result);
    }

    [Test]
    public                              void
Subtract_ReturnsCorrectDifference_WhenGivenTwoN
umbers()
    {
        int result = calculator.Subtract(10, 5);
        Assert.AreEqual(5, result);
    }

    [Test]
    public                              void
Multiply_ReturnsCorrectProduct_WhenGivenTwoNumb
ers()
    {
        int result = calculator.Multiply(3, 5);
        Assert.AreEqual(15, result);
    }
```

```
[Test]
public                                void
Divide_ReturnsCorrectQuotient_WhenGivenTwoNumbe
rs()
    {
        double  result  =  calculator.Divide(10,
2);
        Assert.AreEqual(5.0, result);
    }

    [Test]
public                                void
Divide_ThrowsDivideByZeroException_WhenDividing
ByZero()
    {
        Assert.Throws<DivideByZeroException>(()
=> calculator.Divide(10, 0));
    }
}
```

In this example:

- The `CalculatorTests` class contains several test methods, each designed to test a specific method of the `Calculator` class.
- The `Add`, `Subtract`, `Multiply`, and `Divide` methods are tested with appropriate assertions.

- The
  `Divide_ThrowsDivideByZeroException_WhenDi`
  `vidingByZero` test ensures that dividing by zero throws an exception.

### Step 3: Running the Unit Tests

You can run the tests using **NUnit** or **MSTest** through the Test Explorer in Visual Studio. If you are using NUnit, ensure that the NUnit and NUnit3TestAdapter NuGet packages are installed.

---

*Summary*

In this chapter, we learned about **unit testing** and **Test-Driven Development (TDD)**:

- **Unit testing** ensures the correctness of individual units of code by writing tests to verify their behavior.
- We wrote unit tests in C# using **NUnit** and **MSTest**.
- **Test-Driven Development (TDD)** encourages writing tests before code to improve code quality and ensure correctness.
- We provided a **real-world example** of writing unit tests for a `Calculator` class, demonstrating how to test methods like `Add`, `Subtract`, `Multiply`, and `Divide`.

Unit testing and TDD are powerful techniques that help create robust, reliable software. By testing early and often, you ensure that your code behaves as expected and catch bugs before they become bigger issues.

# CHAPTER 23

# DEPENDENCY INJECTION AND INVERSION OF CONTROL (IOC)

In this chapter, we will explore the concepts of **Dependency Injection (DI)** and **Inversion of Control (IoC)**, which are foundational principles in modern software development. These concepts help manage dependencies between objects, improve the flexibility of your code, and promote loose coupling. We will also explore how **IoC containers** work in C# and demonstrate how to manage dependencies in a real-world **web application**.

*Understanding Dependency Injection (DI)*

**Dependency Injection (DI)** is a design pattern that allows you to inject dependencies (objects) into a class rather than allowing the class to create them internally. This leads to more modular, testable, and maintainable code. DI is a specific type of **Inversion of Control (IoC)**, where the control of creating and managing dependencies is transferred to an external container or framework.

## Benefits of Dependency Injection

1. **Loose Coupling**: Classes are less dependent on concrete implementations, making them easier to change or extend.
2. **Testability**: DI makes it easier to substitute real dependencies with mock or fake dependencies for unit testing.
3. **Maintainability**: DI promotes better separation of concerns and reduces code duplication, making your codebase easier to maintain.

## Basic Example of Dependency Injection

Consider a scenario where a `Car` class depends on an `Engine` class. Instead of the `Car` class creating the `Engine` class internally, we inject the dependency:

```csharp
public class Engine
{
    public void Start()
    {
        Console.WriteLine("Engine started.");
    }
}
```

```csharp
public class Car
{
    private readonly Engine _engine;

    // Dependency Injection via constructor
    public Car(Engine engine)
    {
        _engine = engine;
    }

    public void Drive()
    {
        _engine.Start();
        Console.WriteLine("Car is driving.");
    }
}

class Program
{
    static void Main()
    {
        // Manually creating the Engine and
injecting it into Car
        Engine engine = new Engine();
        Car car = new Car(engine);
        car.Drive();
    }
}
```

In this example:

- The `Car` class does not create an instance of `Engine`; instead, it is passed as a dependency via the constructor.
- This makes the `Car` class easier to test and modify without changing the `Engine` class directly.

---

*Inversion of Control (IoC)*

**Inversion of Control (IoC)** is a broader concept that refers to transferring control of certain operations or decisions from the class itself to a container or framework. DI is one form of IoC, but IoC can also involve other techniques like **Event-based Programming** or **Service Locator** patterns.

In IoC, the framework or container controls the flow of the application, and instead of a class creating or managing its dependencies, the container injects them.

Example of Inversion of Control (IoC)

In traditional programming, a class might control how it gets its dependencies. With IoC, that control is transferred to a container, which is responsible for managing the lifecycle and resolution of dependencies.

*IoC Containers in C#*

An **IoC container** is a framework that manages the lifecycle and dependencies of objects. In C#, there are several popular IoC containers, such as:

- **Microsoft.Extensions.DependencyInjection** (built into ASP.NET Core)
- **Autofac**
- **Ninject**
- **Castle Windsor**

IoC containers handle the creation of objects and the injection of their dependencies. They allow you to configure the dependencies at one central place and resolve them throughout your application, simplifying the management of dependencies.

Example of Using an IoC Container (Microsoft.Extensions.DependencyInjection)

Let's see how to use the built-in IoC container in ASP.NET Core to manage dependencies. This example is applicable for web applications or any application that uses dependency injection.

1. **Step 1: Configure Services in Startup.cs**

In a typical ASP.NET Core application, you configure services (dependencies) in the `ConfigureServices` method of `Startup.cs`.

csharp

```
public class Startup
{
    public                              void
ConfigureServices(IServiceCollection services)
    {
        // Register dependencies with the IoC
container
        services.AddSingleton<Engine>();      //
Singleton instance of Engine
        services.AddScoped<Car>();            //
Scoped instance of Car
    }

    public   void   Configure(IApplicationBuilder
app, IWebHostEnvironment env)
    {
        // Standard ASP.NET Core setup...
    }
}
```

In this example:

- We use `AddSingleton` to register the `Engine` class, which means the same instance will be used throughout the application's lifetime.
- We use `AddScoped` to register the `Car` class, which means a new instance of `Car` will be created per HTTP request (in a web application).

2. **Step 2: Injecting Dependencies in Controllers**

In an ASP.NET Core web application, you can inject dependencies into controllers via constructor injection.

```csharp
public class CarController : Controller
{
    private readonly Car _car;

    // Constructor injection
    public CarController(Car car)
    {
        _car = car;
    }

    public IActionResult Drive()
    {
        _car.Drive();
        return Ok("Car is driving.");
    }
```

```
}
```

In this example:

- The `CarController` depends on the `Car` class, and ASP.NET Core's IoC container automatically injects the `Car` instance into the controller.

---

*Real-World Example: Managing Dependencies in a Web Application*

Let's walk through a more complete real-world example of managing dependencies using DI and IoC in an ASP.NET Core application. We will create a simple **UserService** that depends on a **Database** class, and we'll configure these dependencies using the IoC container.

Step 1: Define the Services and Dependencies
csharp

```
public class Database
{
    public void Connect()
    {
        Console.WriteLine("Connecting    to    the
database...");
    }
```

```
}

public class UserService
{
    private readonly Database _database;

    // Constructor injection of the Database
dependency
    public UserService(Database database)
    {
        _database = database;
    }

    public void CreateUser(string username)
    {
        _database.Connect();
        Console.WriteLine($"User        {username}
created.");
    }
}
```

In this example:

- The UserService depends on the Database class to
  perform operations like connecting to the database.

Step 2: Configure Dependencies in Startup.cs

In the `Startup.cs` file, configure the IoC container to inject the `Database` and `UserService` dependencies.

csharp

```
public class Startup
{
    public                                void
ConfigureServices(IServiceCollection services)
    {
        // Register dependencies with the IoC
container
        services.AddSingleton<Database>();    //
Singleton for the Database
        services.AddScoped<UserService>();    //
Scoped for the UserService
    }

    public   void   Configure(IApplicationBuilder
app, IWebHostEnvironment env)
    {
        // Standard ASP.NET Core setup...
    }
}
```

Step 3: Inject Dependencies in the Controller

Now, we will inject the `UserService` into a controller, which will call its `CreateUser` method.

csharp

```csharp
public class UserController : Controller
{
    private readonly UserService _userService;

    // Constructor injection of the UserService
    dependency
    public          UserController(UserService
    userService)
    {
        _userService = userService;
    }

    public IActionResult Create(string username)
    {
        _userService.CreateUser(username);
        return Ok($"User {username} created.");
    }
}
```

In this example:

- The `UserController` automatically receives an instance of `UserService` through dependency injection.

Step 4: Running the Application

When you run the application and navigate to the `Create` action of `UserController`, it will automatically resolve the `Database` and `UserService` dependencies through the IoC container and perform the operation:

```css
Connecting to the database...
User johndoe created.
```

*Summary*

In this chapter, we explored **Dependency Injection (DI)** and **Inversion of Control (IoC)** in C#:

- **Dependency Injection** allows you to inject dependencies into classes, making the code more modular, testable, and maintainable.
- **Inversion of Control (IoC)** refers to transferring control of object creation and dependency management to an external container.

- We explored how **IoC containers** (such as the built-in container in ASP.NET Core) help manage dependencies in web applications.

- We provided a **real-world example** of managing dependencies in an ASP.NET Core application, where services like `UserService` and `Database` are injected into controllers using DI.

DI and IoC are essential principles in modern software design and are widely used in web frameworks like ASP.NET Core to promote better separation of concerns and modularity.

# CHAPTER 24

# ADVANCED C# FEATURES: NULLABLE TYPES, TUPLES, AND PATTERN MATCHING

In this chapter, we will explore some of the more **advanced features** of C#, including **nullable types**, **tuples**, and **pattern matching**. These features allow you to write cleaner, more efficient, and more readable code. We will discuss each feature, explain how to use them, and provide **real-world examples** to demonstrate how each feature can be applied in practice.

---

## Nullable Types and Null-Coalescing Operators

In C#, variables of value types (like `int`, `double`, `bool`) cannot be assigned `null` by default. However, sometimes you may need a variable of a value type to be able to represent `null`, for example, to handle database values or optional user input. **Nullable types** allow you to store `null` in value types.

C# for Object-Oriented Programming:

## Nullable Types

To define a nullable value type, use the ? modifier after the type. For example, int? is a nullable integer.

csharp

```
int? number = null;
Console.WriteLine(number.HasValue                ?
number.Value.ToString()   :   "No   value");   //
Outputs: No value
```

In this example:

- The int? type allows number to be null.
- The HasValue property checks whether the nullable type has a value.
- If HasValue is true, you can access the value using .Value.

## Null-Coalescing Operator (??)

The **null-coalescing operator** (??) is used to provide a default value when a nullable type is null.

csharp

```
int? number = null;
```

```
int result = number ?? 10;   // If number is null,
return 10.
Console.WriteLine(result);    // Outputs: 10
```

In this example:

- If number is null, the operator returns the right-hand operand (10).

Null-Coalescing Assignment Operator (??=)

Introduced in C# 8.0, the **null-coalescing assignment operator** (??=) assigns a value only if the left-hand operand is null.

csharp

```
int? number = null;
number ??= 10;   // Assign 10 if number is null.
Console.WriteLine(number);   // Outputs: 10
```

This operator simplifies the code when you want to assign a default value to a nullable variable only when it is null.

---

*Working with Tuples*

Tuples are a convenient way to group multiple values together without needing to define a class or struct. C# supports

**immutable tuples**, and they are often used for returning multiple values from methods or representing small data structures.

Creating Tuples

You can create a tuple using the `Tuple` class or the more modern tuple syntax with `ValueTuple`.

csharp

```
// Using ValueTuple
var person = ("John", 30);
Console.WriteLine(person.Item1);    //    Outputs:
John
Console.WriteLine(person.Item2); // Outputs: 30
```

In this example:

- We create a tuple `person` with two elements: a string ("John") and an integer (30).
- `Item1` and `Item2` are automatically assigned the tuple values.

Named Elements in Tuples

Starting from C# 7.0, you can give meaningful names to tuple elements, improving readability.

csharp

```
var person = (Name: "John", Age: 30);
Console.WriteLine(person.Name);    // Outputs:
John
Console.WriteLine(person.Age);   // Outputs: 30
```

In this example:

- The tuple has named elements `Name` and `Age` instead of `Item1` and `Item2`.

Returning Tuples from Methods

You can return tuples from methods to return multiple values.

csharp

```
public (string, int) GetPersonInfo()
{
    return ("John", 30);
}

var person = GetPersonInfo();
Console.WriteLine(person.Item1);    // Outputs:
John
Console.WriteLine(person.Item2);  // Outputs: 30
```

This makes it easy to return more than one value from a method without needing a custom class or struct.

*Pattern Matching in C#*

Pattern matching allows you to match and work with data types more easily in `switch` statements and `if` conditions. C# introduced several types of pattern matching in **C# 7.0**, and enhanced them in **C# 9.0** and later versions.

Type Pattern Matching

One of the most common uses of pattern matching is in `switch` statements or `if` conditions where you need to check the type of an object.

csharp

```
object obj = "Hello, World!";
if (obj is string s)
{
    Console.WriteLine($"The object is a string:
{s}"); // Outputs: The object is a string: Hello,
World!
}
```

In this example:

- We use the `is` keyword to check if `obj` is of type `string`.
- If it is, we assign it to the variable `s` and print it.

Switch Expressions (C# 8.0 and Later)

Switch expressions allow you to write more concise `switch` statements, improving readability and flexibility.

csharp

```csharp
object obj = 42;
string result = obj switch
{
    int i => $"It's an integer: {i}",
    string s => $"It's a string: {s}",
    _ => "Unknown type"
};
Console.WriteLine(result);   // Outputs: It's an integer: 42
```

In this example:

- The `switch` expression evaluates `obj` and matches it to a specific type, returning a formatted string.
- The _ case acts as a default for any type that doesn't match.

Positional Pattern Matching (C# 9.0 and Later)

Introduced in C# 9.0, **positional patterns** allow you to destructure objects, such as tuples or records, directly within a `switch` statement.

293

```
csharp

var point = new Point(3, 4);

string description = point switch
{
    (0, 0) => "Origin",
    (var x, var y) when x == y => "On the line y
= x",
    _ => "Somewhere else"
};

Console.WriteLine(description);    // Outputs:
Somewhere else
```

In this example:

- We use a positional pattern to match the coordinates of the Point object.
- The when clause allows for further filtering based on conditions.

---

*Real-World Examples for Each Feature*

Nullable Types: Handling Optional User Input

Let's assume we have an optional field, like a middle name, that a user may or may not provide.

csharp

```csharp
public void DisplayFullName(string firstName,
string? middleName, string lastName)
{
    string fullName = middleName ?? $"{firstName}
{lastName}"; // If middleName is null,
concatenate first and last name.
    Console.WriteLine($"Full name: {fullName}");
}

DisplayFullName("John", null, "Doe"); //
Outputs: Full name: John Doe
DisplayFullName("John", "William", "Doe"); //
Outputs: Full name: John William Doe
```

In this example:

- We use a nullable `string?` for the `middleName` parameter and the null-coalescing operator to handle the optional middle name.

Tuples: Returning Multiple Values from a Method

Imagine a method that retrieves both a product's name and its price.

csharp

```csharp
public (string productName, decimal price)
GetProductInfo(int productId)
{
    // Simulating a database lookup
    return ("Laptop", 999.99m);
}

var (name, price) = GetProductInfo(1);
Console.WriteLine($"Product: {name}, Price: {price}");
```

In this example:

- The method returns a tuple containing the product name and price.
- The tuple is destructured into `name` and `price` variables for easy access.

### Pattern Matching: Simplifying Object Checks

Consider an application where you need to process different types of messages. With pattern matching, you can simplify your `switch` logic.

csharp

```csharp
public void ProcessMessage(object message)
{
    switch (message)
```

```
    {
        case string s:
            Console.WriteLine($"Received      a
string: {s}");
            break;
        case int i:
            Console.WriteLine($"Received      an
integer: {i}");
            break;
        default:
            Console.WriteLine("Unknown    message
type.");
            break;
    }
}


ProcessMessage("Hello, world!");    // Outputs:
Received a string: Hello, world!
ProcessMessage(42);                 // Outputs:
Received an integer: 42
```

In this example:

- We use **type pattern matching** within a `switch` statement to handle different message types.
- The method processes messages based on their types using the `is` keyword.

*Summary*

In this chapter, we covered three **advanced C# features**:

- **Nullable Types**: Enable value types to represent `null`, making it easier to handle optional or missing data.
- **Tuples**: Allow you to group multiple values together, simplifying the return of multiple values from methods.
- **Pattern Matching**: Simplifies type checks, object destructuring, and conditionally matching patterns, making code more readable and maintainable.

These features are powerful tools that enhance C#'s flexibility, allowing you to write cleaner, more efficient code.

# CHAPTER 25

# WORKING WITH APIS AND WEB SERVICES

In this chapter, we will explore how to interact with APIs and web services in C#. Specifically, we will learn how to make **HTTP requests**, understand the basics of **RESTful APIs**, and work with **JSON** data. We will also provide a **real-world example** of fetching **weather data** from an API.

## Making HTTP Requests in C#

To interact with web services, you'll often need to make HTTP requests. C# provides several ways to send HTTP requests, with the most common being the `HttpClient` class, which is part of the `System.Net.Http` namespace.

## HttpClient Overview

`HttpClient` is a high-level API that simplifies making HTTP requests and receiving responses from a remote server. It supports all common HTTP methods like GET, POST, PUT, and DELETE.

Making a Simple GET Request

**Here's how to make a simple GET request using** `HttpClient`:

csharp

```csharp
using System;
using System.Net.Http;
using System.Threading.Tasks;

class Program
{
    static async Task Main(string[] args)
    {
        string url = "https://api.github.com"; // Example API URL

        using (HttpClient client = new HttpClient())
        {

client.DefaultRequestHeaders.Add("User-Agent", "C# App");

            HttpResponseMessage response = await client.GetAsync(url);

            if (response.IsSuccessStatusCode)
            {
```

```
              string   responseData   =   await
response.Content.ReadAsStringAsync();

Console.WriteLine(responseData);   // Output the
response content
            }
            else
            {
            Console.WriteLine("Error:   "   +
response.StatusCode);
            }
        }
    }
}
```

In this example:

- We create an instance of `HttpClient` to make a GET request to the specified `url`.
- We use `GetAsync()` to send the request asynchronously.
- If the response is successful, we read and output the response content using `ReadAsStringAsync()`.
- The `"User-Agent"` header is required by many APIs (in this case, GitHub's API).

Making POST Requests

To send data in a POST request, you can use the `PostAsync()` method:

301

```csharp
csharp

using System;
using System.Net.Http;
using System.Text;
using System.Threading.Tasks;

class Program
{
    static async Task Main(string[] args)
    {
        string url =
"https://api.example.com/endpoint";
        var data = new { Name = "John", Age = 30
};  // Example data to send

        using (HttpClient client = new
HttpClient())
        {
            string jsonData =
Newtonsoft.Json.JsonConvert.SerializeObject(dat
a);
            var content = new
StringContent(jsonData, Encoding.UTF8,
"application/json");

            HttpResponseMessage response = await
client.PostAsync(url, content);
```

```
        if (response.IsSuccessStatusCode)
        {
            string   responseData   =   await
response.Content.ReadAsStringAsync();

Console.WriteLine(responseData);   // Output the
response content
        }
        else
        {
            Console.WriteLine("Error:   "   +
response.StatusCode);
        }
    }
}
```

In this example:

- We send a POST request with a JSON payload to the specified `url`.
- The data is serialized into JSON format using `Newtonsoft.Json.JsonConvert.SerializeObject()`.
- We use `StringContent` to specify the request body and content type (`application/json`).

*Introduction to RESTful APIs*

A **RESTful API** (Representational State Transfer) is a type of web service that adheres to certain architectural principles:

1. **Stateless**: Each request from the client to the server must contain all the information needed to understand and process the request (i.e., no session data is stored on the server).

2. **Resource-Based**: REST APIs treat everything as a resource that can be accessed or manipulated using standard HTTP methods (GET, POST, PUT, DELETE).

3. **JSON or XML**: RESTful APIs commonly use JSON for data exchange, although XML can also be used.

4. **Uniform Interface**: RESTful APIs expose a consistent set of endpoints (URLs) that represent different operations on resources.

Common HTTP methods used in RESTful APIs:

- **GET**: Retrieve data from the server.
- **POST**: Create a new resource.
- **PUT**: Update an existing resource.
- **DELETE**: Delete a resource.

*Example of RESTful API URL Structure*

A typical RESTful API URL structure might look like this:

```
pgsql

GET /users          -> Retrieves a list of users
GET /users/{id}     -> Retrieves a specific user
by ID
POST /users          -> Creates a new user
PUT /users/{id}      -> Updates an existing user
by ID
DELETE /users/{id}   -> Deletes a user by ID
```

*Real-World Example: Fetching Weather Data from an API*

Let's walk through an example where we fetch weather data from a **public weather API**. For this example, we will use the **OpenWeatherMap API**, which provides weather data for any location. You can get a free API key by signing up on the OpenWeatherMap website.

1. **Step 1: Get an API Key**
   o Go to the OpenWeatherMap website: https://openweathermap.org/api
   o Sign up and get your free API key.
2. **Step 2: Fetch Weather Data**

Here's how to fetch the current weather data for a city using `HttpClient`:

```
csharp
```

```csharp
using System;
using System.Net.Http;
using System.Threading.Tasks;

class Program
{
    static async Task Main(string[] args)
    {
        string city = "London";
        string apiKey = "your_api_key";    // Replace with your actual API key
        string url = $"http://api.openweathermap.org/data/2.5/weather?q={city}&appid={apiKey}&units=metric";

        using (HttpClient client = new HttpClient())
        {
            HttpResponseMessage response = await client.GetAsync(url);

            if (response.IsSuccessStatusCode)
            {
                string responseData = await response.Content.ReadAsStringAsync();
                Console.WriteLine($"Weather data for {city}: {responseData}");
            }
```

```
        else
        {
            Console.WriteLine("Error:    "    +
response.StatusCode);
        }
    }
  }
}
```

In this example:

- We make a GET request to the **OpenWeatherMap API** to fetch the current weather data for a city.
- The `q={city}` query parameter specifies the city, and the `appid={apiKey}` query parameter includes our API key.
- The `units=metric` parameter ensures the temperature is returned in Celsius.
- The `response.Content.ReadAsStringAsync()` method is used to read the JSON response from the API.

Step 3: Parse the JSON Response

The data returned by the API is in JSON format. To work with it in C#, you can deserialize the JSON into an object using a library like **Newtonsoft.Json** (Json.NET).

First, install the **Newtonsoft.Json** NuGet package:

```bash
Install-Package Newtonsoft.Json
```

Now, we can deserialize the JSON response into a C# object:

```csharp
using System;
using System.Net.Http;
using System.Threading.Tasks;
using Newtonsoft.Json;

class Program
{
    public class WeatherData
    {
        public MainData Main { get; set; }
    }

    public class MainData
    {
        public float Temp { get; set; }
    }

    static async Task Main(string[] args)
    {
        string city = "London";
        string apiKey = "your_api_key";    // Replace with your actual API key
```

```csharp
        string              url              =
$"http://api.openweathermap.org/data/2.5/weathe
r?q={city}&appid={apiKey}&units=metric";

        using    (HttpClient   client   =   new
HttpClient())
        {
            HttpResponseMessage response = await
client.GetAsync(url);

            if (response.IsSuccessStatusCode)
            {
                string   responseData   =   await
response.Content.ReadAsStringAsync();
                WeatherData      weather      =
JsonConvert.DeserializeObject<WeatherData>(resp
onseData);

                Console.WriteLine($"Current
temperature in {city}: {weather.Main.Temp}°C");
            }
            else
            {
                Console.WriteLine("Error:    "    +
response.StatusCode);
            }
        }
    }
}
```

In this updated example:

- We define a `WeatherData` class with a `MainData` class to map the structure of the JSON response.
- The `JsonConvert.DeserializeObject<WeatherData>()` method is used to parse the JSON string into a `WeatherData` object.
- We print the current temperature of the city by accessing `weather.Main.Temp`.

*Summary*

In this chapter, we covered how to work with **APIs and web services** in C#:

- **Making HTTP Requests**: We used `HttpClient` to send HTTP requests and handle responses in C#.
- **RESTful APIs**: We discussed the principles of REST and how to interact with RESTful APIs using HTTP methods like GET and POST.
- **Real-World Example**: We demonstrated how to fetch weather data from the **OpenWeatherMap API**, parse the JSON response, and display the temperature for a city.

APIs are an essential part of modern software development, enabling communication between different systems and services. Understanding how to interact with APIs in C# is a crucial skill for building applications that can integrate with external data sources.

# CHAPTER 26

# BEST PRACTICES IN OBJECT-ORIENTED DESIGN

In this chapter, we will discuss the **best practices** in **Object-Oriented Design (OOD)**, focusing on the **SOLID principles**, which are a set of guidelines that help you write clean, maintainable, and scalable object-oriented code. We will also look at how to write clean and maintainable code in general and provide a **real-world example** of refactoring a messy `Order` class to demonstrate these principles.

---

*SOLID Principles*

The **SOLID** principles are five object-oriented design principles that, when followed, lead to more maintainable, flexible, and scalable code. These principles help to reduce dependencies between classes, making your code easier to extend and modify over time.

1. **S**: **Single Responsibility Principle (SRP)**
2. **O**: **Open/Closed Principle (OCP)**
3. **L**: **Liskov Substitution Principle (LSP)**
4. **I**: **Interface Segregation Principle (ISP)**

## 5. D: Dependency Inversion Principle (DIP)

*1. Single Responsibility Principle (SRP)*

The **Single Responsibility Principle** states that a class should have only one reason to change, meaning it should have only one job or responsibility. This leads to smaller, more focused classes that are easier to test and maintain.

Example of Violating SRP

csharp

```csharp
public class Order
{
    public void AddItem(string item)
    {
        // Add item to order
    }

    public void CalculateTotal()
    {
        // Calculate total cost of items in the
order
    }

    public void PrintInvoice()
    {
        // Print invoice for the order
```

```
    }
}
```

In this example:

- The `Order` class violates SRP because it has three different responsibilities: adding items, calculating totals, and printing invoices. If any of these responsibilities change, the `Order` class would need to be modified.

### Applying SRP

To follow SRP, we can break the responsibilities into separate classes:

csharp

```
public class Order
{
    private List<string> items = new
List<string>();

    public void AddItem(string item)
    {
        items.Add(item);
    }

    public List<string> GetItems()
    {
```

```
            return items;
      }
}


public class OrderTotalCalculator
{
    public decimal CalculateTotal(Order order)
    {
        // Calculate total cost based on the
items in the order
        return order.GetItems().Count * 10.0m;
// Example price per item
    }
}


public class InvoicePrinter
{
    public void PrintInvoice(Order order)
    {
        // Print order details
        Console.WriteLine("Printing invoice for
order...");
    }
}
```

Now:

- The Order class is only responsible for managing the items in the order.

315

- The `OrderTotalCalculator` class handles the calculation of the total.
- The `InvoicePrinter` class handles printing the invoice.

Each class now has one responsibility, making the code more modular and easier to maintain.

---

## 2. Open/Closed Principle (OCP)

The **Open/Closed Principle** states that classes should be open for extension but closed for modification. This means you should be able to extend the behavior of a class without changing its existing code.

Example of Violating OCP

csharp

```
public class Order
{
    public    decimal    CalculateDiscount(string
customerType)
    {
        if (customerType == "Regular")
        {
            return  0.05m;    // 5% discount for
regular customers
        }
```

```
        else if (customerType == "Premium")
        {
            return 0.10m;    // 10% discount for
premium customers
        }
        else
        {
            return 0.0m;     // No discount for
unknown customer types
        }
    }
}
```

In this example:

- The Order class needs to be modified if a new customer type with a different discount is added, which violates OCP.

Applying OCP

To follow OCP, we can create an interface for discounts and extend it for different customer types:

csharp

```
public interface IDiscount
{
    decimal GetDiscount();
```

```
}


public class RegularCustomerDiscount : IDiscount
{
    public decimal GetDiscount()
    {
        return 0.05m;  // 5% discount for regular
customers
    }
}


public class PremiumCustomerDiscount : IDiscount
{
    public decimal GetDiscount()
    {
        return 0.10m;   // 10% discount  for
premium customers
    }
}


public class Order
{
    private IDiscount discount;

    public Order(IDiscount discount)
    {
        this.discount = discount;
    }
```

```
public decimal CalculateDiscount()
{
    return discount.GetDiscount();
}
}
```

Now:

- We can add new discount types by creating new classes that implement the IDiscount interface without modifying the Order class.

## 3. Liskov Substitution Principle (LSP)

The **Liskov Substitution Principle** states that objects of a subclass should be able to replace objects of the base class without affecting the correctness of the program. In other words, a derived class must be substitutable for its base class without changing the expected behavior.

Example of Violating LSP

csharp

```
public class Bird
{
    public virtual void Fly()
    {
        Console.WriteLine("Flying...");
```

319

```csharp
    }
}

public class Penguin : Bird
{
    public override void Fly()
    {
        throw                          new
InvalidOperationException("Penguins         can't
fly!");
    }
}
```

In this example:

- The `Penguin` class violates LSP because it cannot substitute `Bird` without changing the expected behavior. If you try to call `Fly()` on a `Penguin` object, it throws an exception.

Applying LSP

To fix this, we can separate the concept of flying from birds that can't fly:

csharp

```csharp
public interface IFlyable
{
```

```
    void Fly();
}


public class Bird { }

public class Sparrow : Bird, IFlyable
{
    public void Fly()
    {
        Console.WriteLine("Flying...");
    }
}


public class Penguin : Bird { }
```

Now:

- Only birds that can fly implement the IFlyable interface, and the Penguin class doesn't need to override the Fly method.

---

*4. Interface Segregation Principle (ISP)*

The **Interface Segregation Principle** states that clients should not be forced to implement interfaces they don't use. This means that interfaces should be small and focused on specific functionality, not large and general.

Example of Violating ISP

csharp

```csharp
public interface IWorker
{
    void Work();
    void Eat();
}

public class Worker : IWorker
{
    public          void          Work()          {
Console.WriteLine("Working..."); }
    public          void          Eat()           {
Console.WriteLine("Eating..."); }
}

public class Robot : IWorker
{
    public          void          Work()          {
Console.WriteLine("Working..."); }
    public   void   Eat()   {   throw   new
NotImplementedException(); }  // Robots don't eat
}
```

In this example:

- The `Robot` class is forced to implement the `Eat()` method, which violates ISP because robots don't need to eat.

Applying ISP

We can break the interface into smaller, more focused interfaces:

```csharp
public interface IWorkable
{
    void Work();
}

public interface IFeedable
{
    void Eat();
}

public class Worker : IWorkable, IFeedable
{
    public void Work() { Console.WriteLine("Working..."); }
    public void Eat() { Console.WriteLine("Eating..."); }
}

public class Robot : IWorkable
```

323

```
{

    public           void           Work()              {
Console.WriteLine("Working..."); }
}
```

Now:

- The `Robot` class only implements the `IWorkable` interface, and `Worker` implements both interfaces. This follows ISP by allowing each class to implement only the functionality it needs.

---

*5. Dependency Inversion Principle (DIP)*

The **Dependency Inversion Principle** states that high-level modules should not depend on low-level modules, but both should depend on abstractions. Furthermore, abstractions should not depend on details, but details should depend on abstractions.

Example of Violating DIP
csharp

```
public class OrderProcessor
{
    private EmailService emailService = new
EmailService();

    public void ProcessOrder(Order order)
```

324

```
    {
        emailService.SendConfirmation(order);
    }
}
```

In this example:

- The `OrderProcessor` class depends directly on the `EmailService` class, which is a low-level implementation. This violates DIP because it tightly couples high-level and low-level modules.

### Applying DIP

We can depend on an abstraction (interface) rather than a concrete implementation:

csharp

```csharp
public interface IEmailService
{
    void SendConfirmation(Order order);
}

public class EmailService : IEmailService
{
    public void SendConfirmation(Order order)
    {
```

325

```
        Console.WriteLine("Sending          email
confirmation...");
    }
}


public class OrderProcessor
{
    private readonly IEmailService emailService;

    public          OrderProcessor(IEmailService
emailService)
    {
        this.emailService = emailService;
    }

    public void ProcessOrder(Order order)
    {
        emailService.SendConfirmation(order);
    }
}
```

Now:

- The `OrderProcessor` class depends on the `IEmailService` interface, not the concrete `EmailService` class. The concrete implementation can be injected at runtime, adhering to DIP.

*Writing Clean and Maintainable Code*

In addition to the SOLID principles, here are some general best practices for writing clean and maintainable code:

1. **Keep Methods Small and Focused**: Each method should do one thing and do it well.

2. **Use Meaningful Names**: Use descriptive variable, method, and class names to make your code self-explanatory.

3. **Avoid Code Duplication**: If you find yourself writing the same code more than once, consider extracting it into a reusable method or class.

4. **Write Unit Tests**: Tests help ensure that your code works as expected and provides documentation for how your code should behave.

*Real-World Example: Refactoring a Messy "Order" Class*

Let's refactor the following messy Order class to follow the SOLID principles.

Original Messy Order Class

```csharp
public class Order
{
```

```csharp
    private List<string> items;
    private string customerName;
    private decimal total;

    public void AddItem(string item)
    {
        items.Add(item);
    }

    public decimal CalculateTotal()
    {
        total = items.Count * 10.0m;   // For
simplicity, assume each item costs $10
        return total;
    }

    public void PrintOrderSummary()
    {
        Console.WriteLine("Order Summary:");
        Console.WriteLine($"Customer:
{customerName}");
        Console.WriteLine($"Total: {total}");
    }

    public void SendConfirmationEmail()
    {
        Console.WriteLine("Sending    email    to
customer...");
    }
```

```
}
```

Refactored Order Class

csharp

```csharp
public class Order
{
    private    List<string>    items    =    new
List<string>();

    public void AddItem(string item)
    {
        items.Add(item);
    }

    public List<string> GetItems()
    {
        return items;
    }
}

public interface IOrderCalculator
{
    decimal CalculateTotal(Order order);
}

public    class    SimpleOrderCalculator    :
IOrderCalculator
{
    public decimal CalculateTotal(Order order)
```

```csharp
    {
        return order.GetItems().Count * 10.0m;
    }
}


public interface IOrderPrinter
{
    void PrintOrderSummary(Order order);
}


public class OrderPrinter : IOrderPrinter
{
    public void PrintOrderSummary(Order order)
    {
        Console.WriteLine("Order Summary:");
        Console.WriteLine($"Items:
{string.Join(", ", order.GetItems())}");
        Console.WriteLine($"Total:
{order.GetItems().Count * 10.0m}");
    }
}


public interface IEmailService
{
    void SendConfirmationEmail(Order order);
}


public class EmailService : IEmailService
{
```

```
    public    void    SendConfirmationEmail(Order
order)
    {
        Console.WriteLine("Sending    confirmation
email...");
    }
}
```

Explanation of Refactoring

- We split the responsibilities into multiple classes: Order, OrderPrinter, EmailService, and OrderCalculator.

- The Order class now only manages items.

- The OrderCalculator, OrderPrinter, and EmailService classes handle specific tasks.

- Each class adheres to the **Single Responsibility Principle**.

- We also used **dependency injection** (DIP) to inject dependencies like IOrderCalculator, IOrderPrinter, and IEmailService into the OrderProcessor class.

---

*Summary*

In this chapter, we explored **best practices in object-oriented design**, focusing on the **SOLID principles**:

- **Single Responsibility Principle (SRP)**
- **Open/Closed Principle (OCP)**
- **Liskov Substitution Principle (LSP)**
- **Interface Segregation Principle (ISP)**
- **Dependency Inversion Principle (DIP)**

We demonstrated how these principles improve code maintainability, testability, and flexibility. We also provided a real-world example of refactoring a messy `Order` class to adhere to these principles, making it easier to maintain and extend.

By following the SOLID principles and general best practices, you can write cleaner, more maintainable code that is easier to understand, modify, and extend over time.

# CHAPTER 27

# BUILDING REAL-WORLD APPLICATIONS WITH C#

In this final chapter, we will take everything we've learned in the previous chapters and put it all together. From the basics of object-oriented programming (OOP) to advanced features like dependency injection, pattern matching, and unit testing, we will now walk through the process of building a real-world application using **C#**. We'll cover everything from **design** to **deployment**, using best practices for writing maintainable and scalable code. To tie it all together, we will also discuss the process of creating a simple project—either a **task manager** or an **e-commerce site**—and conclude with final thoughts on **mastering C# and OOP**.

*Putting It All Together: From Design to Deployment*

Building a real-world application involves several steps, including **planning**, **designing**, **coding**, **testing**, and **deploying**. Let's break down these steps and apply them to a simple project.

## 1. Project Planning and Requirements

Before we start coding, it's important to plan the project and define its requirements. For this example, let's assume we are building a **task manager application**. Here's a list of possible features and requirements:

- **Task Management**: Create, update, and delete tasks.
- **Task Categories**: Categorize tasks (e.g., work, personal).
- **User Authentication**: Allow users to register, log in, and manage their tasks.
- **Due Dates and Priorities**: Set due dates and task priorities (e.g., high, medium, low).
- **Task Status**: Track task completion (e.g., not started, in progress, completed).

Once the requirements are defined, we can begin designing the architecture of the application.

---

## 2. Design: High-Level Architecture

In object-oriented design, we'll use **SOLID principles** to ensure that the system is scalable and maintainable. Here's a simple architecture for our task manager:

- **Models**: Classes representing entities in the system, such as `Task`, `User`, and `Category`.

- **Controllers**: Handle the business logic and interact with the models.
- **Services**: Provide reusable logic, like task sorting, filtering, or sending notifications.
- **Data Access Layer**: Interact with the database (e.g., using Entity Framework for an ORM approach).

High-Level Components

1. **Task Model**: Represents a task in the system.
2. **User Model**: Represents a user, including authentication and user profile information.
3. **TaskService**: Contains logic for creating, updating, deleting, and retrieving tasks.
4. **UserService**: Handles user registration, login, and management.
5. **Database (EF Core)**: Stores task and user data.

*3. Coding the Application*

Let's start by coding the core models and services for the **task manager application**.

Step 1: Task Model
csharp

```
public class Task
```

```csharp
{
    public int Id { get; set; }
    public string Title { get; set; }
    public string Description { get; set; }
    public DateTime DueDate { get; set; }
    public string Priority { get; set; } // e.g.,
Low, Medium, High
    public string Status { get; set; } // e.g.,
Not Started, In Progress, Completed
    public int CategoryId { get; set; }

    public Category Category { get; set; }
}
```

Step 2: User Model

csharp

```csharp
public class User
{
    public int Id { get; set; }
    public string Username { get; set; }
    public string PasswordHash { get; set; } //
Secure password storage
    public string Email { get; set; }
}
```

Step 3: Category Model

csharp

```csharp
public class Category
{
```

336

```csharp
    public int Id { get; set; }
    public string Name { get; set; }  // e.g.,
Work, Personal
}
```

Step 4: TaskService

csharp

```csharp
public class TaskService
{
    private    readonly    ApplicationDbContext
_context;

    public    TaskService(ApplicationDbContext
context)
    {
        _context = context;
    }

    public async Task CreateTaskAsync(string
title, string description, DateTime dueDate,
string priority, int categoryId)
    {
        var task = new Task
        {
            Title = title,
            Description = description,
            DueDate = dueDate,
            Priority = priority,
```

337

```csharp
            Status = "Not Started",  // Default
status

            CategoryId = categoryId
        };


        _context.Tasks.Add(task);
        await _context.SaveChangesAsync();
    }


    public        async        Task<List<Task>>
GetTasksByUserIdAsync(int userId)
    {
        return await _context.Tasks.Where(t =>
t.UserId == userId).ToListAsync();
    }
}
```

Step 5: UserService

csharp

```csharp
public class UserService
{
    private    readonly    ApplicationDbContext
_context;


    public        UserService(ApplicationDbContext
context)
    {
        _context = context;
    }
```

338

```csharp
public        async        Task<User>
RegisterUserAsync(string username, string email,
string password)
    {
        var user = new User
        {
            Username = username,
            Email = email,
            PasswordHash                        =
HashPassword(password)   // Implement password
hashing
        };

        _context.Users.Add(user);
        await _context.SaveChangesAsync();
        return user;
    }

    public        async        Task<User>
LoginUserAsync(string username, string password)
    {
        var        user        =        await
_context.Users.SingleOrDefaultAsync(u        =>
u.Username == username);

        if      (user      ==      null      ||
!VerifyPassword(password,    user.PasswordHash))
// Implement password verification
```

339

```csharp
        {
            return null;  // Invalid login
        }

        return user;
    }
}
```

Step 6: Controllers

The **controller** will be responsible for interacting with the services and returning the appropriate responses to the user.

csharp

```csharp
public class TaskController : Controller
{
    private readonly TaskService _taskService;

    public           TaskController(TaskService
taskService)
    {
        _taskService = taskService;
    }

    public      async      Task<IActionResult>
CreateTask(string   title,   string   description,
DateTime    dueDate,    string    priority,    int
categoryId)
    {
```

```
        await
_taskService.CreateTaskAsync(title, description,
dueDate, priority, categoryId);
        return  RedirectToAction("Index");    //
Redirect to task list
    }
}
```

---

*4. Testing the Application*

Now that we've implemented the core functionality, we need to write **unit tests** to ensure everything works correctly. For example, we can test the `TaskService` to make sure that tasks are being created correctly:

csharp

```
[TestFixture]
public class TaskServiceTests
{
    private TaskService _taskService;
    private ApplicationDbContext _context;

    [SetUp]
    public void Setup()
    {
        // Setup in-memory database for testing
```

```
    var         options        =         new
DbContextOptionsBuilder<ApplicationDbContext>()
        .UseInMemoryDatabase(databaseName:
"TaskManager")
        .Options;
    _context              =         new
ApplicationDbContext(options);
    _taskService            =         new
TaskService(_context);
    }


    [Test]
    public            async           Task
CreateTask_ShouldAddTaskToDatabase()
    {
        await _taskService.CreateTaskAsync("Test
Task", "Test Description", DateTime.Now, "High",
1);

        var       tasks       =         await
_context.Tasks.ToListAsync();
        Assert.AreEqual(1, tasks.Count);
        Assert.AreEqual("Test            Task",
tasks[0].Title);
    }
}
```

In this example:

- We use an **in-memory database** for testing, ensuring that the database operations don't affect production data.
- The test checks whether a task is successfully created and added to the database.

## 5. Deployment

After developing the application and testing it thoroughly, we can deploy it. In a typical **web application** scenario:

1. **Publish the application** using Visual Studio or .NET CLI (`dotnet publish`).
2. **Deploy to a web server**: You can deploy to cloud platforms like **Azure**, **AWS**, or **Google Cloud**, or to a local IIS server.
3. **Set up a database**: For production, use a **SQL Server** or **SQLite** database, and configure the connection strings properly.

## Final Thoughts on Mastering C# and OOP

Building real-world applications is an excellent way to solidify your understanding of **C#** and **Object-Oriented Programming (OOP)** principles. Here are a few key takeaways:

1. **Design Patterns and SOLID Principles**: Applying design patterns and the SOLID principles can help you write clean, maintainable, and scalable code.

2. **Testing**: Unit testing is crucial for ensuring that your code works as expected and for preventing regressions in future development.

3. **Continuous Learning**: Mastery of C# and OOP is a continual process. As you work on more projects, you'll learn new techniques and better ways to structure your code.

C# is a powerful, versatile language, and by mastering it, you will be well-equipped to build a wide range of applications, from simple console apps to complex enterprise-level solutions.